BEHOLD THE MAN

R. Kent Hughes

While this book is designed for the reader's personal enjoyment and profit, it is also intended for group study. A Leader's Guide with Victor Multiuse Transparency Masters is available from your local bookstore or from the publisher.

VICTOR

BOOKS a division of SP Publications, Inc.

WHEATON, ILLINOIS 60187

Offices also in
Whitby, Ontario, Canada
Amersham-on-the-Hill, Bucks, England

Unless otherwise noted, Scripture quotations are from the *New American Standard Bible,* © the Lockman Foundation 1960, 1962, 1963, 1971, 1972, 1973, 1975, 1977. Other quotations are from the *Holy Bible: New International Version* (NIV), © 1978 by the New York International Bible Society. Used by permission of Zondervan Bible Publishers; *The Living Bible* (TLB), © 1971 by Tyndale House Publishers, Wheaton, Ill; the *King James Version* (KJV).

Recommended Dewey Decimal Classification: 226.5
  Suggested Subject Heading: JOHN

Library of Congress Catalog Card Number: 84-50144
ISBN:0-89693-328

VICTOR BOOKS
A division of SP Publications, Inc.
        Wheaton, Illinois 60187

Contents

Foreword

Martin Luther said of the Gospel of John, "This is the unique, tender, genuine, chief Gospel.... Should a tyrant succeed in destroying the Scripture and only a single copy of the Epistle to the Romans and the Gospel according to John escape him, Christianity would be saved."

This is a book on John's Gospel: how to get into it for study and how to go out from it for living. Kent Hughes deals first with the text—and then he deals with us.

Pastor Hughes is a man who both reads and thinks. How privileged we are to get in on his studies! As I read the manuscript myself, I marked many pages as I thought, "This is good.... I want to keep that." I plan to pass on these insights myself, with the hope that others may also be stimulated and enriched.

> *Father, as this particular reader moves into this book, open his or her mind to own personally the truths here shared. Through Christ our Lord, Amen.*

Raymond C. Ortlund
Corona del Mar, California

1

The Delays of Love

John 11:1-44

Sometimes you may think that God just doesn't care about you. The circumstances of your life don't seem to allow for any other explanation. When you are being ravaged by the events of your life, it is very difficult to believe that God's silences and delays are really evidences of His love. And yet they often are. If you find yourself with the questions that Mary and Martha asked of Jesus, then with them you may find some answers to your difficult circumstances.

Jesus' Delay

There was an emergency in Bethany at the house of Jesus' friends, Mary, Martha, and Lazarus. Lazarus was very sick and his sisters sent word to Jesus, who was in the wilderness with His disciples. They were sure He would come right away to heal their brother. For Jesus was a special friend of theirs, and He had chosen to make their home a place where He could rest and be at home. Yes, He would surely come to Bethany.

The word they sent to Jesus was, "Behold, he whom You love is sick" (John 11:3). The word they used for love is *phileo*, meaning close friendship.

But when Jesus received the news, He said:

> "This sickness is not unto death, but for the glory of God, that the Son of God may be glorified by it" (11:4).

When John commented on Jesus' reaction, he used another word for love, *agape,* that unstoppable and highest form of love:

> Now Jesus loved Martha, and her sister, and Lazarus. When therefore He heard that he was sick, He stayed then two days longer in the place where He was (11:5-6).

How was staying put an evidence of the highest love? We can understand this only if we can learn to see from God's perspective. For only then will we see His inexplicable delays as delays of love. Because we can never comprehend God's workings in their completeness, we need to look through the eyes of faith.

For two days Jesus went about His work, far away from the anguished sisters, while they were going through a hell on earth. Each hour they must have looked outside to see if Jesus were approaching, and then gone back to be with Lazarus, whose life was ebbing away.

At the end of two days, Jesus told His disciples that they were returning to Judea. Their friend Lazarus had fallen asleep, and He wanted to wake him from his sleep.

> The disciples therefore said to Him, "Lord, if he has fallen asleep he will recover."
> Now Jesus had spoken of his death; but they thought that He was speaking of literal sleep.
> Then Jesus therefore said to them plainly, "Lazarus is dead, and I am glad for your sakes that I was not there, so that you may believe; but let us go to him."
> Thomas therefore, who is called Didymus, said to his fellow disciples, "Let us also go, that we may die with Him" (11:12-16).

Thomas expressed the pessimism that many of the disciples must have felt. They knew that people in Judea were seeking to stone Jesus, and here He was heading right back into the middle of things—to visit a dead man!

Some Hard Questions

In Bethany, after Lazarus had died and his sisters had risen up from his bed, a cry went up from that house to the streets around. They prepared Lazarus for burial, putting on him a white linen gown poignantly called a traveling dress, and wrapping him lovingly with bandages and spices. Then the women led a procession out to the tomb. Women always walked ahead in funeral processions, since it was prejudicially believed that since the woman first sinned, death came through her.

At the grave there were memorial speeches, and then the mourners lined both sides of the path and wailed as the sisters passed through toward their home.

By the time Jesus was on His way to Bethany, it was the fourth day, when the ritual of mourning had reached its highest point—by now the body was decaying, and there was no hope.

Mary and Martha heard that Jesus was close by. Martha, deciding to go out to meet Him, made her way to the edge of town. There she stood—pale, grieving, weary, disheveled. Behind her was the Palestinian countryside with its heat. In front of her, heavy with the dust of travel, were Jesus and His men.

Martha's greeting to Jesus was, "Lord, if You had been here, my brother would not have died!" (11:21) I think she and Mary had said something like this many times in the past several days. The wait had been agonizing, as they had wondered, "When is the Lord going to get here?" Martha's words were almost a reproof to Him, but then she caught herself and said, "Even now I know that whatever You ask of God, God will give You" (11:22).

Have you ever felt as Martha did? "Lord, where were You? Lord, You are too late. Where were You when my loved one died? Where were You when my marriage dissolved? Where were You when my parents divorced? Where were You when my father became an alcoholic? Where were You when I was cheated of my promotion? Where were You when my child went wrong?"

Jesus did not reprove Martha for her words. It is not sinful to tell God how you feel. Yes, you should retain reverence toward God, but that does not mean you cannot express to Him your deepest emotions.

Many people have a misconception about Christianity—that "good Christians" should not cry or express their inner feelings. How wrong can we be! King David sorrowed and was disillusioned. He told God his feelings and God did not reprove him. The Prophet Habakkuk poured out his complaint to God.

Now Martha had done the same thing. Notice her conversation with Jesus:

> Jesus said to her, "Your brother shall rise again."
> Martha said to Him, "I know that he will rise again in the resurrection on the last day" (11:23-24).

It is as if she were saying, "I know, of course. But, Lord, what about now?"

Then Jesus responded with what we know as the sixth great "I AM" statement in the Gospel of John:

> "I am the resurrection, and the life; he who believes in Me shall live even if he dies, and everyone who lives and believes in Me shall never die. Do you believe this?" (11:25-26)

Martha answered with her great confession:

> "Yes, Lord, I have believed that You are the Christ, the Son of God, even He who comes into the world" (11:27).

Here was a remarkable woman of faith, one of Jesus' favorite people. We have to face the fact that even the most spiritual people suffer difficulties. They suffer the delays of love.

Jesus Cares

While Jesus and Martha were talking, Mary was back at the house, where all the furniture was turned around, in keeping with funeral tradition. As William Barclay informs us, the mourners were sitting either on the floor or on low stools they had brought. After the sisters had returned from the grave, earlier in the day, they had all eaten a traditional meal of lentils, boiled eggs, and round loaves of bread. By their shape, the loaves symbolized that life was rolling on to eternity (William Barclay, *The Gospel of John,* vol. 2, Westminster Press, pp. 103-104).

I rather suspect that Mary had not eaten much since that meal. She too was probably disheveled in appearance, because mourners were committed to not washing themselves or wearing sandals, and this was the fourth day of mourning.

Martha now left Jesus and went back to find Mary. She said to her, "The Teacher is here, and is calling for you" (11:28). Mary quickly got up and started toward where Jesus was. The mourners in her house didn't know where she was going. Assuming that she was returning to the tomb, they followed her.

When Mary came to the place where Jesus was, she fell at His feet and said, "Lord, if You had been here, my brother would not have died" (11:32). There is that refrain again, the mourning song on their lips. Jesus looked at Mary and at all the mourners following her, and as He felt their sorrow, "He was deeply moved in spirit, and was troubled" (11:33).

The word for "deeply moved" comes from an ancient Greek word that describes a horse snorting. When taken in context here, it implies that our Lord let out an involuntary gasp. The breath just went out of Him. E.V. Rieu translates the thought, "He gave way to such distress of spirit as made His body tremble" (*The Four Gospels,* Emile Victor Rieu, Penguin Books, p. 225). Our Lord was so caught up in the sisters' emotion that He gasped. He felt their sorrow with everything He had. And He voluntarily took Mary and Martha's sorrows to His heart.

[Jesus] said, "Where have you laid him?" They said to Him, "Lord, come and see." Jesus wept (11:34-35).

Jesus did not wail. The word used here means that the tears ran down His face. Here we see a picture of the great God who loves us, who delays and stays away, who allows us to go through the ultimate extremity, and then comes and enters into our sorrows. He enters them in such a way that He gasps; His whole being shudders, and then He weeps with us.

If you are hurting, He wants you to know that He weeps with you. Jesus is not a stoic, impassible God. Neither is God the Father. In Hebrews we read, "He [Jesus] is the radiance of His glory and the exact representation of His nature" (Heb. 1:3).

In the opening verses of his Gospel, John wrote:

> No man has seen God at any time; the only begotten God, who is in the bosom of the Father, He has explained [exegeted] Him (1:18).

In other words, Jesus is the exegesis of God. Somehow the eternal Father shares in our sorrows. We do not have a high priest who cannot be touched with the feelings of our infirmities. We can know that when we pour our hearts out to Him, He comes and sorrows with us.

Dancing on Death

Watching Jesus' reactions, some of the mourners said, "Behold, how He loved him!" Others said, "Could not this man, who opened the eyes of him who was blind, have kept this man also from dying?" (11:36-37)

They all walked to where Lazarus was buried. A tomb of that day was a hollowed-out room in a hillside or cave, with space for eight bodies. When they got there, Jesus asked that the stone be rolled away.

> Jesus therefore again being deeply moved within, [that is, the involuntary shudder] came to the tomb. Now it was a cave, and a stone was lying against it. Jesus said, "Remove the stone."
> Martha, the sister of the deceased, said to Him, "Lord, by this time there will be a stench, for he has been dead four days" (11:38-39).

We can understand how Martha felt. With all this misery,

why open the grave and let the stench come out? Why look at the face of a putrefying corpse? She did not understand what Jesus wanted to do.

Jesus said to her, "Did I not say to you, if you believe, you will see the glory of God?" And so they removed the stone. And Jesus raised His eyes, and said, "Father, I thank Thee that Thou heardest Me. And I knew that Thou hearest Me always; but because of the people standing around I said it, that they may believe that Thou didst send Me" (11:40-42).

Picture the scene. The stone was rolled away. They all could see Lazarus' body, and possibly more bodies. Then the people grew more quiet as they looked to Jesus with a sense of expectation. His eyes were aglow as He cried out, "Lazarus, come forth!"

As the crowd stared into that tomb, they saw movement. They saw Lazarus' body edge off the stone, then stand erect and emerge mummy-like into the sunlight. The mourners saw Mary and Martha feverishly begin to unwrap him. And then they were all part of the biggest carrying-on, as they wept over him, hugged him, and danced about in their bare feet. The funeral had become a festival.

Love's Delays

What is God's word to us in this story? For we know that some problems are never solved on this earth. We know that our dead are not brought back to us now. There are three words for our comfort.

The first word is resurrection. When Martha spoke of the future day of resurrection, she was referring to the time about which the Apostle John wrote:

And He shall wipe away every tear from their eyes; and there shall no longer be any death; there shall no longer be any mourning, or crying, or pain; the first things have passed away (Rev. 21:4).

The second word is in the compassion Jesus felt for the sorrows of His friends, as He entered into their deepest hurts.

And the third word is one that comes to us from the Apostle Paul:

> And we know that God causes all things to work together for good to those who love God, to those who are called according to His purpose" (Rom. 8:28).

As an exile and prisoner in Egypt, Joseph experienced more pain and injustice and deprivation than most of us do. But years later he was able to say about it, "God meant it for good" (Gen. 50:20).

How we respond to the sorrows of life depends on our perspective. If we believe that God is in control, then we will see His delays as delays of love. We will know His silences as silences of love.

He wants us to ask Him the big questions. He wants us to pour out our hearts to Him. He is not an impassible, stoic God, but One who feels with us and weeps in our weeping. He understands us better than we understand ourselves. He brings joy and resurrection life out of our extremity. And in our pain, He works out His purposes for good.

2
A Forever Family Portrait

John 11:47—12:11

After Jesus raised Lazarus from the dead, the Jewish religious authorities were in a dilemma. Jesus was already popular with the people. Now they were afraid that everyone would believe in Him. If that happened, the Romans just might decide to take away the privileges of the religious rulers and even prevent Israel from functioning as a nation.

They did not know where to turn for a solution until Caiaphas, the high priest, came to their aid. He was a Sadducee, which meant that he did not believe in the resurrection, either present or future. He collaborated with the Romans and didn't want anyone rocking the boat, especially some peasant from Galilee.

Caiaphas had been high priest for sixteen years. He was intellectual, cynical, and ruthless. Note the cunning in his words to the council:

> "You know nothing at all, nor do you take into account that it is expedient for you that one man should die for the people, and that the whole nation should not perish" (John 11:49-50).

Roughly translated, he said, "You fools! If you had any intelligence at all, you would see that the answer is simple. Far better that one should die than that a whole nation should die."

15

Capable, self-sufficient, shrewd, an ecclesiastical climber, Caiaphas had arrived at the top of his profession. Yet even Caiaphas was not fully in control. He would have been amazed had he later seen the commentary of the Apostle John on his statement to the council:

> Now this he did not say on his own initiative; but being high priest that year, he prophesied that Jesus was going to die for the nation; and not for the nation only, but that He might also gather together into one the children of God who are scattered abroad (11:51-52).

The council accepted Caiaphas' unintended prophecy of the vicarious atonement of Jesus and "from that day on they planned together to kill Him" (11:53).

The Passover was at hand and in Jerusalem the very air was electric. There were tense conversations everywhere, some loud, others in careful tones: "Do you think He is really going to come to the Passover?"

"No, I don't think He will chance it."

"Well, I do."

On the sixth day before Passover—when our Lord would give His life on the cross—He approached Jerusalem.

> Jesus, therefore, six days before the Passover, came to Bethany where Lazarus was, whom Jesus had raised from the dead. So they made Him a supper there, and Martha was serving; but Lazarus was one of those reclining at the table with Him (12:1-2).

From the Gospels of Matthew and Mark we learn that the supper was in the house of Simon the Leper and that the disciples were all there. So we know that the table was set for at least seventeen. This dinner was a celebration, a thank-you to Jesus for Lazarus' resurrection. It had to be a time of great joy. And yet it was also a brave action for the host; for when the authorities found out about it, they would be unhappy with him.

The dinner included the people who had been the closest to Jesus, those whose lives had been changed by Him. We want to concentrate on the family of Bethany—Martha, Mary, and Lazarus—for in each of them we can see an aspect of worship to our Lord.

Serving Is Worship

Martha served this dinner and she must have been in her element. Even as a guest in Simon's home, she was in charge of the kitchen. She had probably stayed up the night before, getting things ready, and then had been up early on this special day to bake the meat and the breads. All day the aroma of a celebration meal had wafted through the rooms of the house. Nothing was too good for Jesus!

This meal reminds us of another one, not too long before, when Martha and Mary had entertained Jesus in their home. You remember how Mary had gone in to talk with Jesus, leaving Martha in the kitchen by herself to finish the meal. And Martha had become more and more irked until she had said to Jesus, "Lord, don't You care for me? Tell Mary to come back out here and help me." And Jesus had answered her:

> "Martha, Martha, you are worried and bothered about so many things. . . . Mary has chosen the good part, which shall not be taken away from her" (Luke 10:41-42).

What an embarrassing time that had been for both Mary and Martha. But at this dinner in Simon's home, things were different. Martha seemed at peace. What had happened to her?

Circumstances had not changed, but Martha had. She had not mistaken what the Lord said. For He did not tell her to become a Mary, and it is a good thing, because if she had, they probably would have starved!

Martha understood Jesus to mean that her harried and unhappy attitude was separating her from Him and from peace. Now she had learned that even in her serving she could be worshiping. For true worship involves service. When Paul wrote to the Romans, he told them to present their bodies as their spiritual service of worship (12:1). Preparing a meal can be worship. Taking a test can be worship. Administering a business can be worship.

Catherine Booth was the wife of the founder of the Salvation Army. She was also a woman of immense gifts who had a remarkable public ministry. Her son wrote about her healthy understanding that all of life can be offered to God as a form of worship:

> She began her public ministry when I, her eldest child, was five years old. But her own home was never neglected for what some would call—I doubt whether she would have so described it— the larger sphere. Both alike had been opened to her by God. She saw His purposes in both. In the humble duties of the kitchen table, her hands busy with the food, or in the nursery when the children were going to bed, or at the bedside of a sick child, she was working for God's glory (Bramwell Booth, *These Fifty Years,* London: Cassell and Company, 1929, p. 25).

No matter if she ministered publicly or at home, Catherine Booth realized it was all worship and work for God. Martha had learned that lesson between the two dinners. In preparation for this second one, her spirit was right, so that her service was akin to the dramatic outward worship of Mary after the meal.

The options are always before us—we can complain about those who are not doing their jobs the way we think they should. We can be sour. Or we can do our work lovingly and gently. We can each realize that we are accountable to God for our own service. Those whose hearts have been touched by Christ are usually faithful in loving service, regardless of what others do.

I saw this kind of service several years ago. It was in 1976 that I sat in the living room of a proud, accomplished man and watched as the tears coursed down his face. We had been talking about his need for Jesus as Saviour and he said to me, "I'll take Him if He will have me."

From my point of view, Big Jim's conversion was a miracle. He was a hard-driving, self-sufficient man. His father had been with Thomas Edison the night they activated the incandescent bulb and he later became one of the founders of the Southern California Edison Company. Big Jim had spent forty years as an executive with that company.

Jim's conversion was real, but the roughness was still there. It took him months to stop using an expletive when he complimented something that happened at church. At times he was completely unreasonable and gave me grief. Yet his life was changed, and he wanted to serve Christ.

We were in a building program, and even though Jim lived thirty miles from the church, he made the trip almost every day so that he could work on the building. The fondest memory I have of Big Jim is of him outside the church on a hot, smoggy August afternoon. He was sitting cross-legged over the controls of a sprinkling system we were installing and I was urging him to go back home and go to bed, since he had a history of heart trouble (which claimed his life in just a few weeks).

Jim told me that afternoon, "Pastor, with what Christ has done for me, I just can't do enough for Him." This is the mark of those who have truly had their lives touched by Christ. This is what we see in Martha.

Giving Is Worship

As the celebration progresses, we turn our attention to Mary. She left the table and then returned with a container of valuable ointment.

> Mary therefore took a pound of very costly, genuine spikenard-ointment, and anointed the feet of Jesus, and wiped His feet with her hair; and the house was filled with the fragrance of the ointment (12:3).

Mary's giving to Jesus was very costly. Judas estimated the value of the spikenard at about 300 denarii, and a denarius was one day's wage. Calculated in our money, at a wage of $8 an hour, the ointment would have been worth just over $19,000. Poured out on Jesus' feet!

Mary's question to herself had been, "What can I do to show that I love Jesus?" In her giving, she lavished love on Jesus, and He did not reject her. She gave her most treasured possession. But then, Martha did too, for she valued work; and her gift to Jesus was just as noble as Mary's expensive ointment.

What is your most valued possession or ability? Whatever it is, will you make it available to Jesus? Mary humbly gave Him her best. She got down on her knees and loosed her hair. A woman's hair was symbolic of her glory, and Mary lavished Jesus with her glory. She was self-forgetting and passionate.

I do not see the Lord restraining Mary, just as He did not restrain the prostitute who had performed a similar act some time earlier (Luke 7). Of Mary's action He said, "She has done a beautiful thing" (Matt. 26:10, NIV).

John tells us that the house was filled with the fragrance of the perfume. Mary didn't try to give a small portion of what she valued. Rather she gave all to Jesus. When she bent over Jesus' feet and wiped the perfume away with her hair, she then had the fragrance of the gift on her person. Her unself-conscious and worshipful act made her a means of spreading the fragrance of Christ.

If your life doesn't make other people think of Jesus, if your days seem dry and unprofitable, you need to do what Mary did—get down on your knees before Him and give Him all of what you value most. Pour out your life before Him.

Judas viewed Mary's gift differently than did the others at the meal. He said, "Why was this ointment not sold for three hundred denarii, and given to poor people?" (12:5) This sounded very impressive, as if Judas were really sensitive to the needs of the poor. Actually, he was using high-sounding words to disguise his greed, for Judas was a thief.

> Now he said this, not because he was concerned about the poor, but because he was a thief, and as he had the money box, he used to pilfer what was put into it (12:6).

Mary and Judas stand in extreme contrast. She was selfless,

giving, believing. Judas was selfish, greedy, and unbelieving. To the person who has never met God, the worship that gives all seems the most impractical, wasteful pursuit in life. Jesus' response to Judas was:

> "Let her alone, in order that she may keep it for the day of My burial. For the poor you always have with you; but you do not always have Me" (12:7-8).

Many people believe that Mary understood Christ's approaching death more clearly than the others who knew Him. In this respect G. Campbell Morgan wrote, "I would rather be in succession to Mary of Bethany than to the whole crowd of the apostles" (*The Gospel According to John,* Fleming H. Revell, p. 208).

Living Is Worship

As the celebration moved on into the evening, more and more people arrived at the home of Simon. They wanted to see Jesus and especially Lazarus.

> The great multitude therefore of the Jews learned that He was there; and they came, not for Jesus' sake only, but that they might also see Lazarus, whom He raised from the dead. But the chief priests took counsel that they might put Lazarus to death also; because on account of him many of the Jews were going away, and were believing in Jesus (12:9-11).

Lazarus had become Jesus' star witness, and yet Lazarus never said or did anything worth recording. But his very life was a form of witness and worship, not because of what Lazarus did for Jesus but because of what Jesus had done for Lazarus.

This speaks to us, because all our serving and all our giving are not going to mean anything unless we have experienced in a spiritual way what Lazarus did in physically coming back to life. We need to hear the voice saying, "Come forth," and we need to be unbound from what keeps us from freedom. For when we are free, we become unanswerable arguments for

Christ—with lives so changed that the only way they can be accounted for is the power of Christ.

Lazarus reminds us of the reason we worship. Mary is a picture of pouring out all that we have in selfless worship. Martha is a portrait of worshipful service. And together they make a remarkable picture of what Jesus does when He touches our lives.

Do you want your life to be a fragrance before God and to others? Then look to the family portrait from Bethany—of Lazarus with his new life and fellowship with Christ; of Mary at the feet of Jesus pouring out her most valued treasure; and of Martha as she served, offering the energy of her life to Him. And then hold this picture before you as a challenge of what you can be.

3
Regal Living

John 12:12-26

On December 4, 1977 in Bangui, capital of the Central African Empire, the world press witnessed the coronation of his Imperial Majesty, Bokassa I. The price tag for that one event, designed and choreographed by French designer Olivier Brice, was $25 million. At 10:10 that morning, the blare of trumpets and roll of drums announced the approach of His Majesty. The procession began with eight of Bokassa's twenty-nine official children parading down the royal carpet to their seats. They were followed by Jean Bédel Bokassa II, heir to the throne, dressed in admiral's white with gold braid. He was seated on a red pillow to the left of the throne. Catherine, the favorite of Bokassa's nine wives, followed. She was wearing a $73,000 gown made by Lanvin of Paris, strewn with pearls she had picked out herself.

The Emperor arrived in a gold, eagle-bedecked imperial coach drawn by six matched Anglo-Norman horses. When the Marine Band blared, "The Sacred March of His Majesty, Emperor Bokassa I," His Highness strode forth, cloaked in a thirty-two-pound robe decorated with 785,000 pearls and gold embroidery. White gloves adorned his hands, pearl slippers his feet. On his brow he wore a gold crown of laurel wreath like those worn by Roman consuls of old, a symbol of the favor of the gods.

As "The Sacred March" came to a conclusion, Bokassa seated himself on his $2.5 million eagle throne and took his gold laurel wreath off. Then, as Napoleon had done 173 years before, Bokassa crowned himself. His crown, also valued at $2.5 million, was topped with an eighty-carat diamond. The twentieth century had a new emperor.

Bokassa's reign was not as imposing as his coronation. Just two years later, while he was out of the country, the French engineered a successful coup.

The story of Bokassa's coronation is almost comical. But at the same time, it is a painfully accurate portrayal of the longings and methods of man left to himself to pursue his own exaltation. And this story offers a vivid contrast to the story we have before us about another king.

Presentation of the King

As the Passover approached, the atmosphere in Jerusalem was tense. The rulers of the Jews had decided that Jesus must be eliminated to save the nation. We might think that He would stay away from the city, but He didn't.

> On the next day the great multitude who had come to the feast, when they heard that Jesus was coming to Jerusalem, took the branches of the palm trees, and went out to meet Him, and began to cry out, "Hosanna! Blessed is He who comes in the name of the Lord, even the King of Israel."
> And Jesus, finding a young donkey, sat on it; as it is written, "Fear not, daughter of Zion; behold, your King comes sitting on a donkey's colt" (John 12:12-15).

Hosanna was an anticipatory cry that literally meant "Save" or "Save us" or perhaps "Lord, save Him," similar to "God save the Queen." The people viewed Jesus as their deliverer. Their words, taken from Psalm 118, had been used 100 years before in a political demonstration as Judas Maccabaeus had driven the Greeks out of Acra. The palm branches the people held also had political significance. The palm was the symbol on the coin of the second Maccabean revolt; the waving palm branches represented their nationalistic spirit. The crowd fully expected that Jesus would issue a call to arms and drive out the hated Romans.

Amid all this tumult, Jesus quoted from the words of the Prophet Zechariah, which had been written 500 years previously.

> Rejoice greatly, O daughter of Zion!
> Shout in triumph, O daughter of Jerusalem!
> Behold, your king is coming to you;
> He is just and endowed with salvation,
> Humble, and mounted on a donkey,
> Even on a colt, the foal of a donkey. (Zech. 9:9)

In accord with Zechariah's words, Jesus had directed His disciples to a donkey that had never been ridden. His entrance into Jerusalem on this donkey was purposeful, as He identified Himself with the long-awaited Messiah. Yet in the very simplicity of the act He was showing that He was not like other rulers of the world. The donkey was a royal beast, but it was also an animal of peace. This Jesus who entered the city on a donkey was a new kind of king, one the people could not understand or appreciate, for they wanted a king with a sword. Even His disciples failed to see the significance of Jesus' actions until after His resurrection!

> These things His disciples did not understand at the first; but when Jesus was glorified, then they remembered that these things were written of Him, and that they had done these things to Him (12:16).

As the crowds rushed after Jesus, the religious rulers of the people watched and then said to each other, "You see that you are not doing any good; look, the world has gone after Him" (12:19).

Pursuit of the King

Within the crowds of people approaching Jerusalem were some foreigners arriving for the feast.

> Now there were certain Greeks among those who were going up to worship at the feast; these therefore came to Philip, who was from Bethsaida of Galilee, and began to ask him, saying, "Sir, we wish to see Jesus." Philip came and told Andrew; Andrew and Philip came, and they told Jesus (12:20-22).

The presence of Greeks at the Passover was not unusual. The Greeks were inveterate wanderers. In fact, they were the first people to wander just for the sake of wandering. One Greek chided his own people saying, "You Athenians will never rest yourselves nor will you even let anyone else rest." They were characteristically seekers after truth. It was not unusual for a Greek to go through philosophy after philosophy in his search. If they were alive today, they would probably be armed with cameras and tape-recorders to chronicle their search. They wanted to know. The force of the Greek verb behind "they wanted to see Jesus" is continuous. The idea is that they kept repeating, "Sir, we wish to see Jesus. Won't you take us to see Jesus? Sir, we want to see this man."

I believe that John included the Greek visitors in this story so that we would see Gentiles as part of this uniquely Jewish celebration. After Jesus' birth, wise men from the East came to worship Him. Now, before His death, wise men from the West had come to see Him.

As Jesus began to speak, a hush of expectancy surely fell over the people. His initial words were, "The hour has come for the Son of man to be glorified" (12:23). The hearts of the people must have thrilled. Some of them would have thought of Daniel who was going to set up a worldwide dominion that would not pass away. Surely now Jesus would announce His campaign against the Romans and set Himself up. However, His next words were a great disappointment to them:

"Truly, truly, I say to you, unless a grain of wheat falls into the earth and dies, it remains by itself alone; but if it dies, it bears much fruit" (12:24).

Proclamation by the King

A different kind of hush settled on the crowd as they heard these words. Jesus was talking about a king who would rule through death, not through conquest. His metaphor was so simple. You can hold a kernel of wheat in your hand and yet not see what is inside of it. For each grain contains a million similar offspring. In planting season, a grain is cast forth into the ground, as if into a tomb. There it dies and is set free from its encasement so that it can begin to grow. This drama is enacted a trillion times each year and yet we don't see it happen. We see its results.

Jesus was announcing to the people that He would exercise His kingly role by dying and thereby reproducing His life. That was how He was going to rule, and His rule would extend far beyond the reach of any earthly kingdom. For He would rule not by compulsion but by gaining an allegiance of the heart.

Jesus expanded the principle in these words: "He who loves his life loses it; and he who hates his life in this world shall keep it to life eternal" (12:25). He was not advocating a hatred of life. Rather He was stating the paradoxical principle that we find life only when we lose it for His sake. Whether in this world or in the world to come, our potential is never reached except through death and denial. Self-denial is the key to unlock our potential in life.

Once after Paderewski had finished a brilliant concert, he was told by an admiring woman, "Sir, you are a genius."

To which he responded, "Madam, before I was a genius, I was a drudge." His brilliance came through a kind of death, through hard work and self-denial.

Jim Ryun, the famous runner who set a mile record when he was eighteen years old, talked about his training: "I would run until I felt I couldn't take another step. Then I would run until I felt my lungs were going to burst. When I came to that state, then I would run until I thought I was going to pass out. When I did this, I was making progress."

The eminent H.P. Liddon, while preaching in St. Paul's on Palm Sunday in 1881, said:

> The errors and miseries of the world are purged with blood; everywhere in the great passages of human history we are on the track of sacrifices; and sacrifice, meet it where you may, is a moral power of incalculable force (H.P. Liddon, *Passiontide Sermons*. London: Longmans, Green, and Company, 1903, p. 105).

The spiritual life is governed by similar paradoxes. Do you want to be strong? Then you need to become weak. The Lord told Paul, "Power is perfected in weakness" (2 Cor. 12:9).

Do you want to be rich? You are to become poor. Do you want to be first? You are to be last. To be exalted? "Humble yourselves, therefore, under the mighty hand of God, that He may exalt you at the proper time" (1 Peter 5:6). Do you want to rule? Then you have to serve. Do you want to live? Then you have to die.

Jesus warned that there is great peril in escaping the death of which He spoke. "Truly, truly, I say to you, unless a grain of wheat falls into the earth and dies, it remains by itself alone" (12:24). Unless there is a death, the vast possibilities inside of you will not be released. You will shrivel and remain alone.

Whether you are beginning the Christian life or are awakening to your spiritual potential, you need to learn that you live by dying. Two verses that challenged me in this regard are Romans 12:1-2:

> I urge you therefore, brethren, by the mercies of God, to present your bodies a living and holy sacrifice, acceptable to God, which is your spiritual service of worship. And do not be conformed to this world, but be transformed by the renewing of your mind, that you may prove what the will of God is, that which is good and acceptable and perfect.

Taking this challenge, I gave myself to Christ the best I knew how at the age of twelve, and my life began to grow. And as the years have passed, I have seen that dying is a daily requirement for spiritual vitality. If your life is stagnant, if your spiritual potential is going unrealized, it may well be that you need to die to yourself, lay down your life, and be released.

Someone came to George Mueller one day and asked, "What has been the secret of your life?" Mueller hung his head and said, "There was a day when I died." Then he bent lower and said, "Died to George Mueller, his opinions, preferences, tastes, and will; died to the world, its approval or censure; died to the approval or blame even of brethren or friends."

Death brings a princely life. The principle is still true for us. The kind of power, of reign and royalty that death brings to life, will make the pretenders of this world green with envy.

Jesus summed up self-denial in one sentence: "If anyone serves Me, let him follow Me" (12:26). But if we follow Him from this point, we arrive at Calvary. For the royal life does not begin with a coronation but with a crucifixion. Death to self. But what is the reward? "Where I am, there shall My servant also be; if any one serves Me, the Father will honor him" (12:26).

It has been said that "Follow Me" is the sum of our duty. That "Where I am" is the sum of our reward. And ultimately it means untold honor. The time is coming when our coronation is going to make the world's coronations look like children at play. Paul wrote of this to the Corinthians:

Momentary light affliction is producing for us an eternal weight of glory far beyond all comparison (2 Cor. 4:17).

. . .the wisdom which none of the rulers of this age has understood; for if they had understood it, they would not have crucified the Lord of glory; but just as it is written,
   Things which eye has not seen and ear has not heard, and which have not entered the heart of man, all that God has prepared for those who love Him (1 Cor. 2:8-9).

A story is told of a train of slaves being led along in northern Africa, chained to one another at the neck. As they walked, the Arab slave traders and masters noticed that all of them were bent over with the heavy iron collars—except one. He walked erect and with dignity. One trader said, "Who is he?"

"He's the son of a king and he cannot forget it," was the answer. We too are royalty. We are potential princes, queens, and kings, eligible for sublime honor and glory. The question is: Do we live that royal life now? We do so only in proportion to how we emulate the King of kings.

On that first Palm Sunday when our Lord marched into Jerusalem, the crowds acclaimed Him. The Gentiles came and asked, "We would see Jesus." And how did they see Him? Through His death. How did they understand Him as King? Through His death.

How does the world see Jesus today? Only as we die to ourselves. Let God lead you to a royal life of sacrifice that bears much fruit for His kingdom.

4

On Being People of the Towel

John 13:1-17

As we progress through the Gospel of John, the shadow of the Cross grows longer and darker, for we have come to the eve of the Crucifixion. In less than a day our Lord is going to be suspended between heaven and earth as the Sin-bearer for mankind. Before the sun sets again, He will have breathed His last tortured breath and completed the agony.

Our Lord's public ministry is now over. There will be no more public discourses. Chapters 13—17 record what we know as the Upper Room Discourse. Some people believe this section to be the most sacred in all Scripture, and they call chapter 17 the Holy of Holies. In these five chapters we see the most intimate teaching about service, love, the Holy Spirit, heaven, our union with Christ, and prayer. Alexander Maclaren eloquently gave his estimation of the chapters:

> Nowhere else do the blended lights of our Lord's superhuman dignity and human tenderness shine with such lambent brightness. Nowhere else is His speech at once so simple and so deep. Nowhere else have we the heart of God so unveiled to us. On no other page, even of the Bible, have so many eyes, glistening with tears, looked and had the tears dried. The immortal words which Christ spoke in that upper chamber are His highest

self-revelation in speech" (*Exposition of Holy Scripture*, Baker Book House, vol. 10, p. 171).

The Upper Room Discourse begins with a dramatic call to follow Christ's example as a servant. If we are to be His followers, we need certain qualities in our lives and have to perform certain acts. We will look at the servant of Christ from these directions—his heart, his example, and his challenge.

The Heart of the Servant

Now before the Feast of the Passover, Jesus knowing that His hour had come that He should depart out of this world to the Father, having loved His own who were in the world, He loved them to the end (John 13:1).

The servant's heart is a heart of love. A story about Czar Nicholas I of Russia tells something of that love. The Czar was greatly interested in a young boy because he had been friends with the boy's father. When the young man came of age, Nicholas gave him a fine position in the army and stationed him in one of the great fortresses of Russia, making him responsible for the monies of a division of the army.

The young soldier did quite well at first, but as time passed, he became a gambler. It was not long before he had gambled his entire fortune away. Then he borrowed from the treasury and gambled that away, a few rubles at a time. One day he heard that there would be an immediate audit of the books. He went to the safe, took out his ledger, and figured out how much money should be in the division's accounts. Then he subtracted the amounts that he had taken and discovered he had an astronomical debt. As he sat at the table with the accounts, he took out his pen and wrote, "A great debt, who can pay?" Not willing to face the shame of the next day, he got out his revolver and pledged that at the stroke of midnight he would take his life. It was a warm evening, and as he sat at the table, he dozed off.

Czar Nicholas had a habit of putting on a common soldier's

uniform and visiting his outposts. On that very night he came to the great fortress. As he inspected, he saw a light on in one of the rooms. He knocked at the door but no one answered. He tried the latch, then opened the door and went in. There was the young man to whom he had given so much.

When the Czar saw the note on the table and the ledgers open, his first impulse was to wake the soldier and arrest him. But he was overtaken with a wave of generosity. He picked up the pen that had fallen from the soldier's hand and wrote something under the words the soldier had penned in despair.

About an hour later the soldier woke up and reached for his revolver. As he did, his eyes fell on the paper where he saw, "A great debt, who can pay? Nicholas." He dropped the gun, ran to the files and thumbed through the correspondence to find the Czar's signature. When he did, he saw that it was authentic. Then he realized that the Czar had been there and knew his guilt, and that the Czar had taken the debt on himself so that the soldier would not have to die. The young man trusted in the Czar's word, and sure enough, the money soon arrived (James Boice, *Commentary on John,* vol. 4, pp. 22-24, quoting H. A. Ironside, *Illustrations of Bible Truth,* Zondervan, pp. 67-69).

The Czar's love was an atoning love, as he paid the price for his guilty young friend. But it was only a faint shadow of the atoning love of Christ. Nicholas' act does him great credit and yet it was relatively easy for him, as easy as signing his name and then sending some money. The atoning love of Jesus cost Him everything.

The very tenses used in verse 1 mean that in the whole range of Christ's contact with His disciples, He loved them. "Having loved His own who were in the world, He loved them to the end." And here, in the Upper Room, Christ would make that love the overriding issue:

"A new commandment I give to you, that you love one another, even as I have loved you, that you also love one another. By this all men will know that you are My disciples, if you have love for one another" (13:34-35).

Teaching His people to love was one of Jesus' overall purposes in the Upper Room Discourse. What He was saying to them was this: "If you want to be servants, if you want to grow in this authentic aspect of discipleship, then you have to open yourselves to the possibility of having your hearts deepened in love. Is that what you really desire? Are you willing to grow in love?"

There is another aspect of the Saviour's heart that we must see. Jesus knew exactly who He was. Notice the parallel thoughts in verses 1 and 3 of John 13:

> Jesus knowing that His hour had come that He should depart out of this world. . . .

> Jesus, knowing that the Father had given all things into His hands, and that He had come forth from God, and was going back to God. . . .

It was not that Jesus forgot He was God and so humbled Himself. Rather, being fully conscious of His supremacy and coming exaltation, He became Lord of the towel!

The Example of the Servant

The world was locked out and the disciples were alone with Jesus. Because they were eating the Passover meal, they were reclining in the traditional posture, each with his left arm supporting his head and his right arm free to reach the dishes on the table. Each man's feet were stretched out behind him away from the table.

As they reclined and finished the meal, Jesus rose from the table and began to perform the last labor of His life. The self-conscious, purposeful drama of His act, and the natural intensity it evoked, leads me to believe that there must have been a few murmurs and whispers, and then silence.

Our translation of the story is in the past tense. But the story in the Greek is in the present. Jesus "rises from supper," just as in the Incarnation He rose from His place of perfect fellowship with God the Father and the Holy Spirit. He "lays aside His garments," as He once temporarily set aside His glorious existence. He "takes a towel," just as He once took the form of a servant. He "girds Himself," as He came to earth to serve. He "pours water into the basin," as He was soon to pour out His blood for the washing away of human sin. And He "washes His disciples' feet," just as He cleanses all who are His own.

Jesus had perfectly portrayed His ministry, from birth to death to resurrection to glorification. It is the same epic that we see in Philippians 2:5-9:

> Have this attitude in yourselves which was also in Christ Jesus, who, although He existed in the form of God, did not regard equality with God a thing to be grasped, but emptied Himself, taking the form of a bondservant, and being made in the likeness of men. And being found in appearance as a man, He humbled Himself by becoming obedient to the point of death, even death on a cross. Therefore also God highly exalted Him, and bestowed on Him the name which is above every name.

We can almost hear the uncomfortable quietness in the Upper Room, during which all were aware of the gentle pouring of the water and the friction of the towel and the Master's breathing as He moved from disciple to disciple. As Jesus toweled the feet of Thomas, maybe He thought, "These feet will be beautiful on the mountains." When He came to Judas, "These feet will soon steal away in the dark." Then He came to a pair of 13Ds— Peter's feet. Peter said:

> "Lord, do You wash my feet?"
> Jesus answered and said to him, "What I do you do not realize now; but you shall understand hereafter."
> Peter said to Him, "Never shall You wash my feet!" (13:6-8)

Good old Peter. Sometimes it seemed that the only time he opened his mouth was to change feet. The Greek makes his protestation even more forceful. "Lord, You, my feet do You wash? No, never shall You wash my feet until eternity." Footwashing was a servant's job and Jesus was the Master. According to the Midrash Mekilta on Exodus 21:2, footwashing could not be required of a Hebrew slave (Raymond E. Brown, *The Gospel According to John, XIII—XXI,* Doubleday, p. 564).

Jesus answered Peter, "If I do not wash you, you have no part with Me." Realizing the finality of Jesus' words, Peter exclaimed, "Lord, not my feet only, but also my hands and my head" (13:9).

I like Peter. He would have understood Emerson's sentence: "A foolish consistency is the hobgoblin of little minds, adored by little statesmen and philosophers and divines. With consistency a great soul has simply nothing to do." Peter could change his mind in an instant when it was desirable or necessary.

Jesus' answer referred to the ceremonial laws of the Jewish people, in which a person who was already clean only needed to have his feet washed on arriving at another home to be considered clean. And He gave the custom a spiritual meaning:

> Jesus said to him, "He who has bathed needs only to wash his feet, but is completely clean; and you are clean, but not all of you." For He knew the one who was betraying Him; for this reason He said, "Not all of you are clean" (13:10-11).

As believers, the disciples did not need a radical new cleansing. Rather they needed a daily cleansing from the contaminating effects of sin picked up in their walk through life. When Jesus finished washing the feet of the last one, He rose and put on His garments and again reclined at the table. This reminds us of the words from Hebrews 1 that speak of Christ rising to heaven and joining His Father: "When He had made purification of sins, He sat down at the right hand of the Majesty on high" (Heb. 1:3).

The Challenge of the Servant
Jesus had one question for His disciples: "Do you know what I have done to you?" It seems that they knew and that they were having a difficult time accepting the lowly level of His

service to them. For in Luke's account of the Upper Room we read, "There arose also a dispute among them as to which one of them was regarded to be greatest" (Luke 22:24). With the Cross only a few hours away, the disciples were still arguing over matters of pride. They were willing to fight for the throne, but no one wanted the towel. Then Jesus said:

> "You call Me Teacher and Lord; and you are right; for so I am. If I then, the Lord and the Teacher, washed your feet, you also ought to wash one another's feet. For I gave you an example that you also should do as I did to you. Truly, truly, I say to you, a slave is not greater than his master; neither one who is sent greater than the one who sent him" (13:13-16).

Jesus was employing the compelling logic of a legal *a fortiori* argument: "If it is true for the greater, how much more for the lesser!"

In 1970 I was among 12,300 delegates to Inter-Varsity's Urbana convention, where we heard John Stott give a masterful application of the truth of this passage, as he told the story of Samuel Logan Brengle:

> In 1878 when William Booth's Salvation Army had just been so named, men from all over the world began to enlist. One man, who had once dreamed of himself as a bishop, crossed the Atlantic from America to England to enlist. He was a Methodist minister, Samuel Logan Brengle. And he now turned from a fine pastorate to join Booth's Salvation Army. Brengle later became the Army's first America-born commissioner. But at first Booth accepted his services reluctantly and grudgingly. Booth said to Brengle, "You've been your own boss too long." And in order to instill humility into Brengle, he set him to work cleaning the boots of the other trainees. And Brengle said to himself, "Have I followed my own fancy across the Atlantic in order to black boots?" And then as in a vision he saw Jesus bending over the feet of rough, unlettered fishermen. "Lord," he whispered, "You washed their feet: I will black their boots" (John Stott, *Christ the Liberator*, InterVarsity Press, p. 25).

If we count ourselves followers of Christ, we must have elements of humble service in our lives. We must be people of the towel. This means most specifically that we are to do service for the people of God. This is sometimes more difficult than serving those outside the church. To serve those in our own families where there is no glory—those we know so well and who know us intimately—this is the hardest service of all.

Yet serving those close to us has a cleansing effect on other believers. The impact of Jesus' words is this: The church has received the essential cleansing by Him in the forgiveness of sins. But we can help to take away the day-to-day dirt of the world by humbly serving one another. As we serve each other, we encourage one another to godliness. For the church to attain holiness in the sight of God, it is necessary that many of its members are often engaged in lowly service one to the other, service as lowly and as essential as Christ's washing of the disciples' feet.

However, cleansing is dirty work. If we are going to be part of this approach toward holiness, we are going to get our hands dirty. And this goes against the grain in most of us. So, how do we become people of the towel? There are three factors that enter in.

First, we need the heart of the servant, as Jesus had. He was overflowing with love for His own: "Having loved His own who were in the world, He loved them to the end" (13:1).

Second, we are to follow the example of Christ the servant: "For I gave you an example that you also should do as I did to you" (13:15).

And third, we need to know who we are, as people of the towel. When Jesus said, "Do you know what I have done to you?" He might have added, "And do you know who you are, as heirs to the towel?" The power, the impetus, and the grace to wash one another's feet is proportionate to how we see ourselves. Our Lord saw Himself as King of kings, and He washed their feet. Recovery of a consciousness that we serve Christ the King will also compel us to service.

Jesus' final word to them about lowly service was this: "If you know these things, you are blessed if you do them" (13:17). We don't need to learn more about humble service—we need to do it. Have you joined the Order of the Towel?

5
Radical Love
John 13:18-35

The longest night in the history of the world is drawing to a close. The night is passing, but the day has not yet come. Far to the east, over the mountains of Moab, there is just the faintest intimation of the coming day. The huge walls of Jerusalem and the towers and pinnacles of the Temple are emerging from the shadows of the night. In the half darkness and half light I can make out a solitary figure coming down the winding road from the wall of Jerusalem toward the gorge of the Kedron. On the bridge over the brook he pauses for a moment and, turning, looks back toward the Holy City. Then he goes forward for a few paces and, again turning, halts and looks up toward the massive walls of the city. Again he turns, and this time he does not stop. Now I can see that in his hand he carries a rope. Up the slope of Olivet he comes and, entering in at the gate of Gethsemane, walks under the trees of the Garden. Seizing with his arms one of the low-branching limbs of a gnarled olive tree, he draws himself up into the tree. Perhaps he is the proprietor of this part of the Garden, and has come to gather the olives. But why with a rope? For a little he is lost to my view in the springtime foliage of the tree. Then, suddenly, I see his body plummet down like a rock from the top of the tree. Yet the body does not reach the ground, but is suspended in mid-air. And there it swings slowly to and fro at the end of a rope (Clarence Edward Macartney, *Great Nights of the Bible,* Abingdon-Cokesbury, pp. 86-87).

The setting remains the Upper Room, where Jesus was closeted with the Twelve. And because we know what they did not, our focus settles on Judas. It is midnight for him, and never again will he awaken to the sunshine of Christ's daily fellowship. But even in this last hour, he is the recipient of Christ's radical love.

Love's Demonstration

When Jesus had concluded washing the disciples' feet and had explained the meaning of what He had done, He said:

> "Truly, truly, I say to you, a slave is not greater than his master; neither one who is sent greater than the one who sent him. If you know these things, you are blessed if you do them" (John 13:16-17).

And He may have lowered His voice as He began His next words:

> "I do not speak of all of you. I know the ones I have chosen; but it is that the Scripture may be fulfilled, 'He who eats My bread has lifted up his heel against Me' " (13:18).

What He was saying was, "Men, not all of you are blessed, because there is one here who is going to lift up his heel—the very heel I have just washed—against Me in betrayal." Jesus used a phrase from Psalm 41:9 as He spoke of the betrayer. It is generally agreed that Psalm 41 refers to the traitor Ahithophel who turned against King David (2 Sam. 16—17). As Ahithophel betrayed David and then took his own life, so Judas would now betray the Son of David and then take his own life. Jesus was telling the Twelve, "Men, there is an Ahithophel in our fellowship."

As Jesus' spirit moved toward the awful events that lay ahead, He wanted those He loved to know something of what would occur, so that they would not lose faith:

"From now on I am telling you before it comes to pass, so that when it does occur, you may believe that I am He. Truly, truly, I say to you, he who receives whomever I send receives Me; and he who receives Me receives Him who sent Me" (13:19-20).

When He got to this point, His voice must have given Him away, because John described Him as "troubled in spirit" as He said to them, "Truly, truly, I say to you, that one of you will betray Me" (13:21). The word *troubled* is the same used to describe Jesus when He stood by Lazarus' grave and wept, and again in John 12:27, as He thought of the coming dread of the Cross.

The disciples could see His emotion but did not know that it was because of Judas. Our Lord was troubled, not for Himself but for Judas, the very one who would deliver Him to death. Notice the response of the disciples. They "began looking at one another, at a loss to know of which one He was speaking" (13:22). Matthew records that they were confused: "Lord, is it I? It can't be! Lord, who is it?"

Judas must have coolly mouthed the same words: "Lord, who is it? Who would do such a thing?" He was as perfect an actor, as consummate a hypocrite as could be found. Theologians surmise that Judas was a man of more education and higher social standing than the rest of the disciples. He was not from Galilee but came from Kerioth, a much better address. Dr. Harry Ironside said of him, "Judas was the real gentleman of all the teachers." Compared to the rest, he had class. If Judas were here today, he would know all the hymns and the ritual. He would know when to inject the appropriate Scripture or saying, and when to ingratiate himself with the right word. If Judas were here, we would not suspect him of being a traitor, any more than those in the Upper Room did.

Jesus never raised an eyebrow, never did anything to cast suspicion in Judas' direction, for He was still reaching out to him. When He referred to Psalm 41:9 about Ahithophel, He was again saying, "Judas, old friend, why don't you turn around?" Even the way the seating was arranged demonstrated Jesus' love. John was on one side of Jesus and Judas was on the other. Jesus' head was at Judas' breast as they reclined together. Jesus had given Judas the left-hand side, the place of honor. Maybe He had even walked with him into the meal and had said, "Judas, I want to talk with you. Sit here in the place of honor tonight."

> The disciples began looking at one another, at a loss to know of which one He was speaking. There was reclining on Jesus' breast one of His disciples, whom Jesus loved [John]. Simon Peter therefore gestured to him, and said to him, "Tell us who it is of whom He is speaking." He, leaning back thus on Jesus' breast, said to Him, "Lord, who is it?"
> Jesus therefore answered, "That is the one for whom I shall dip the morsel, and give it to him." So when He had dipped the morsel, He took and gave it to Judas, the son of Simon Iscariot (13:22-26).

In the culture of that time, to take a morsel from the table, dip it in the common dish and then offer it to someone else, was a gesture of special friendship. In the story of Ruth we read of this. Boaz invited Ruth to come and fellowship with him and he said, "Come here, that you may eat of the bread and dip your piece of bread in the vinegar. . . . And he served her" (Ruth 2:14).

Jesus' gesture said, "Judas, here is My friendship. Here is My restoration for you, My heart of love. All you have to do is take it."

But the door was slammed shut. Matthew records Judas' words: "Surely it is not I, Rabbi?" And Jesus responded, "You have said it yourself" (Matt. 26:25).

> And after the morsel, Satan then entered into him. Jesus there-fore said to him, "What you do, do quickly." Now no one of those reclining at table knew for what purpose He had said this to him. For some were supposing, because Judas had the money box that Jesus was saying to him, "Buy the things we have need of for the feast"; or else, that he should give something to the

poor. And so after receiving the morsel he went out immediately; and it was night (13:27-30).

It was certainly the midnight of Judas' soul—a night that would know no morning. Judas had chosen his own place of darkness and doom. As he left the Upper Room, I wonder if he did not pause and look back longingly at the Light. How alone he was and would be in the next hours, as he shadowed Jesus and the other disciples. And how great his loss, as he separated himself from the apostolic fellowship. He was separated from peace of mind. The soul-anguish which made him a suicide was an earnest of what was to come, when he would someday meet Christ at the Judgment.

> The tissues of the life to be,
>   We weave with colors all our own;
> And the fields of destiny,
>   We reap as we have sown.
>   Clarence Macartney,
>   *Great Nights of the Bible*, p. 76

Judas was a victim of his own dark heart. He bore responsibility for what he did, for his deeds were his own. Yet in a way, when he took his life, he was a victim of Jesus' radical love.

Love's Demand

It is this radical love of Jesus which makes the rest of our text intelligible. With Judas gone, it seems that our Lord felt relieved. We have all experienced this. In the presence of someone who doesn't like us, we feel stifled, unable to say what we would like to. But when that person leaves, the conversation flows more easily. And now, even though Jesus was speaking of the Cross, the conversation seems brighter, for the one plotting evil has gone:

When therefore he had gone out, Jesus said, "Now is the Son of man glorified, and God is glorified in Him; if God is glorified in Him, God will also glorify Him in Himself, and will glorify Him immediately. Little children, I am with you a little while *longer*. You shall seek Me; and as I said to the Jews, 'Where I am going, you cannot come,' now I say to you also" (13:31-33).

Because He would no longer be with them, He had a command, a demand of love, for them:

"A new commandment I give to you, that you love one another, even as I have loved you, that you also love one another. By this all men will know that you are My disciples, if you have love for one another" (13:34-35).

Jesus called this a new commandment, although the commandment to love was as old as the Mosaic revelation. He called it new because His radical love demanded a new object and a new measure.

• The new object was "one another." The Jews of Jesus' day had watered down the Mosaic teaching of loving one's neighbor so that they could love or hate whomever they wanted. Christ changed the object from neighbor to one another. He said that those who are His followers are to love one another.

This was a radical new commandment in a world so divided by prejudicial crevasses that many of our modern-day differences look pale by comparison. There was the division between master and slave, the gulf between Jew and Gentile. The Greeks regarded the Jews as barbarians. The Jews had the reputation of being the haters of the world. Also, there was the vast chasm between man and woman. The world of that day seemed helplessly divided. Alexander Maclaren described the effect of Christ's new command:

Barbarian, Scythian, bond and free, male and female, Jew and Greek, learned and ignorant, clasped hands and sat down at one table, and felt themselves all one in Christ Jesus. They were ready to break all other bonds, and to yield to the uniting forces that streamed out from His Cross. There never had been anything like it. No wonder that the world began to babble about sorcery, and conspiracies, and complicity in unnameable vices. It was only that the disciples were obeying the new commandment, and a new thing had come into the world—a community held together by love and not by geographical accidents or linguistic affinities, or the iron fetters of the conqueror. . . . The new commandment made a new thing, and the world wondered (*Expositions of Holy Scripture*, Baker Book House, vol. 10, p. 228).

It was as brothers and sisters that the church conquered the world. We must keep this ever before us. It was a glorious band of brothers and sisters that sailed the oceans and marched through the continents to both dungeon and throne with the Good News. One of the reasons they succeeded is that mankind, severed from one another and longing to come together, witnessed real love among the followers of Christ. This was especially noticeable among the Jews who were the narrowest, most bigoted, most intolerant nation on the face of the earth. Wherever the church succeeds today, it is in large measure due to the love that exists between brothers and sisters in Christ.

Several years ago, Johanne Lukasse, of the Belgian Evangelical Mission, came to the realization that evangelism in Belgium was getting nowhere. The nation's long history of traditional Catholicism, the subsequent disillusionment resulting from Vatican II, and the aggression of the cults, had left the land seemingly impervious to the Gospel.

Driven to the Scriptures, Lukasse read John 13:34-35 and devised a plan. First, he gathered together a heterogeneous group of Belgians, Dutch, and Americans—whoever would come. Second, he had them rent a house and live together for seven months. Naturally, frictions developed as the believers rubbed each other the wrong way. But this friction sent them to prayer and ultimately to victory and love. Then they went out and began to see amazing results as people came to Christ. Outsiders called them "the people who love each other."

Christ's commandment calls us to love all kinds of people, not just those who are like us. Left to ourselves, we seek our own kind. But when Christ comes, that changes. And the greater the love of the new object—one another, the greater the diversity within the body of Christ.

• In His commandment, Christ set a new measure for their love, "as I have loved you." In these words we see the command's radical nature. While it is admittedly difficult to love your neighbor as yourself, it is far more requiring to love others as Christ loves them. This is sacrificial love. And here we see the basis for Christ's dealings with Judas during the hours before the betrayal.

When Jesus told the disciples to love one another "as I have loved you," the Eleven naturally thought of Jesus stooping to wash their feet. But they were at a disadvantage, for they did not then know how Jesus was reaching in love to Judas. We do, though, and can see how Jesus extended the possibility of reconciliation to Judas.

To follow the measure of the command means that we too will reach out in reconciliation, love, and forgiveness to those who are wronging us. When this happens, the world sees a great argument for the validity of the Gospel. "By this all men will know that you are My disciples, if you have love for one another" (13:35).

Perhaps the greatest gift that we as the body of Christ can give the world is our love for our brothers and sisters in Christ. And as we so love, we will help to prepare those on the outside to receive the gift of gifts, the King of kings. God give us such radical love!

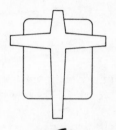

6
Let Not Your Heart Be Troubled
John 14:1-6

We live in an age of heart trouble. A good title for the late twentieth century would be The Cardiac Age. In 1973, 1,060,000 people died of heart ailments. In that year, 54 percent of all deaths were related to the heart (*Heart Facts*, American Heart Association, p. 9).

A substantial factor in the incidence of heart disease is stress. We only need to watch television or read the daily paper to know why—small and large wars, the arms buildup, starvation in some sections of the world, the advance of communism, just for starters. Add to this the change in morals and ethics in our own society, the high divorce rate, the stress of life in a youth-oriented culture.

Within ourselves we find the tendency to borrow trouble, to imagine things as worse than they are. The poet Keats spoke of this: "Imaginary grievances have always been my torment more than real ones." Which is worse, the actual injection in the dentist's chair or the hour before the fact?

In our world we have real reasons for troubled hearts and Christians are not immune. And yet to us, as well as to the disciples, Jesus said, "Let not your heart be troubled" (John 14:1). He used a picturesque word so that His real meaning was, "Don't let your heart shudder." In John 13:21, the same word was used to describe Jesus' emotion as Judas went astray. It is a strong word that would apply specifically to the disciples in the hours that lay ahead of them, when it would seem that the world was falling in, that all was lost, and that darkness would engulf them.

"Let not your heart be troubled"? How do you do that? The prescription follows: "Believe in God, believe also in Me" (14:1). The way to have an untroubled heart is to believe in God and in Jesus whom He sent. The verb tenses used here say, "Keep on believing in God and keep on believing in Me." And at this crucial moment in their lives, Jesus had something specific in mind that He wanted the disciples to believe about Himself and His Father.

Believe in an Eternal Place

"In My Father's house are many dwelling places; if it were not so, I would have told you; for I go to prepare a place for you." (14:2).

We all long for heaven. An effective guard against a troubled heart is to believe that God is preparing an eternal place for us as individuals.

During World War II, a perpetually barefoot little girl walked one day across the grass of a housing project to attend a Good News Club. She had a dream that she thought she could make come true. The teacher of the club, Mrs. White, had promised her a little book called a Wordless Book, and the girl had dreamt about the colored pages in the book. She had encouraged her older brothers and sisters to repeat over and over again the words that went with the pages. The black page stood for sin (Rom. 3:23). The red page was for the blood of Christ (John 3:16). The white page stood for the snow-whiteness of a heart cleansed by God (Isa. 1:18). The gold page stood for the streets of the city in which Christians will live eternally (Rev. 21:21). That afternoon the little girl, my wife Barbara, recited her Bible verses and received a Wordless Book from Mrs. White. Barbara and the rest of the children sang:

My heart was black with sin,
until the Saviour came in;
His precious blood, I know
has washed it white as snow.
And in His Word I'm told
I'll walk the streets of gold;
Oh, wonderful, wonderful day,
He washed my sins away!

Barbara will never forget that day, for it was when she met Jesus as her Saviour. In retrospect, she says that what really drew her was the gold page of the book. It was the promise of a place prepared for her that drew her to Jesus. We all have this longing for heaven. C.S. Lewis wrote of this "inconsolable longing" in *The Problem of Pain:*

> There have been times when I think we do not desire heaven, but more often I find myself wondering whether in our heart of hearts, we have ever desired anything else. . . . It is the secret signature of each soul, the incommunicable and unappeasable want, the thing we desired before we met our wives or made our friends or chose our work, and which we shall still desire on our deathbeds when the mind no longer knows wife or friend or work (Macmillan, pp. 145-147).

Whether people know it or not, they long for a place with Christ. We see it in utopian political philosophies. Marxism at its core feeds on a longing for heaven, even while it thrives on economic woe and political injustice.

Jesus tells us how our unsatisfied longings will be fulfilled: "In My Father's house are many dwelling places." There are permanent dwelling places for us, and in this fact is comfort in trouble, and a rest for our restless hearts.

Psychologists tell us that if when we were children, we did not experience a secure home, it is very likely that as we go through life, we will not feel at home. On the other hand, if as youngsters we were secure and at home, then wherever we go will be home.

If we have this deep, underlying heart realization that there is an eternal abode for us, it will bring rest to our souls in the midst of the troubled world. I believe that this is what made the Apostle Paul such a powerful force in a world that was falling apart. He knew God's sustaining power and, also, he had seen a glimpse of the heavenly places. He spoke of this as if it had happened to someone else, yet the consensus is that he was talking about himself:

> I know a man in Christ who fourteen years ago—whether in the body I do not know or out of the body I do not know, God knows—such a man was caught up to the third heaven. And I know how such a man—whether in the body or apart from the body I do not know, God knows—was caught up into Paradise, and heard inexpressible words, which a man is not permitted to speak (2 Cor. 12:2-4).

Paul himself did not know if this was in a vision or a physical experience. But he did know the spiritual reality of being caught up into Paradise and seeing heavenly realities and hearing the words ineffable that could not be expressed. I believe it was this confidence of a sure place prepared for him that kept him victorious through an amazing list of difficulties, some of which he lists in 2 Corinthians 11.

Paul's perspective on our home in heaven is beautifully expressed in Philippians 3:20: "For our citizenship is in heaven, from which also we eagerly wait for a Saviour, the Lord Jesus Christ." In Ephesians 2:6 we read that we are seated with Christ in the heavenly places.

In this troubled world, the reality of our heavenly abode should guard our hearts. This future home should be in our dreams. It should be as real as anything else in life.

Believe That Christ Is Coming for You

> "If I go and prepare a place for you, I will come again, and receive you to Myself; that where I am, there you may be also" (14:3).

Our comfort is not only in the place; it is also in the presence of Jesus. The words, "I will come again," are in the present tense and really say, "I am coming again." In the New Testament, there are 318 allusions or direct references to the return of the Lord. He is going to take us to be with Him and we will see Him face to face. First John 3:2 speaks of this:

Beloved, now we are children of God, and it has not appeared as yet what we shall be. We know that, when He appears, we shall be like Him, because we shall see Him just as He is.

John Donne responded to this reality with these words:

I shall be so like God that the devil himself shall not know me from God. He will not be able to tempt me any more than he can tempt God. Nor will there be any more chance of my falling out of the kingdom than of God being driven out of it (*Donne's Sermons*, ed. Logan Pearsall Smith, Oxford: Clarendon Press, 1919, p. 228).

The assurance of the kingdom explained why Paul wrote:

I do not know which to choose. But I am hard-pressed from both directions, having the desire to depart and be with Christ, for that is very much better (Phil. 1:22-23).

John 14:1-6 is one of the most comforting of all Scriptures. It is possible that more tears have fallen on John 14 than on any other passage. Dr. A.C. Gabelein used to say that among his family treasures was a German Bible that went back many generations. He said that when he opened to some pages, the Bible looked like new; but at John 14, the pages were spotted, soiled, and worn from the tears of many generations.

The great preacher John Watson said that when a member of his flock was dying and almost ready to expire, sometimes he would kneel down next to the person and whisper, "In My Father's house are many mansions." He might turn away and then come back and hear the person repeating, "Father's house . . . many mansions."

The biography of the Puritan preacher, Henry Venn, says this of his dying moments:

> The prospect made him so high-spirited and jubilant that his doctor said that his joy at dying kept him alive a further fortnight (quoted by John R.W. Stott, *Christ the Liberator,* InterVarsity Press, p. 37).

We are to take great comfort in the fact that Jesus is coming back to take us to be with Himself. Paul wrote to the Thessalonians about this comfort:

> But we do not want you to be uninformed, brethren, about those who are asleep, that you may not grieve as do the rest who have no hope. For if we believe that Jesus died and rose again, even so God will bring with Him those who have fallen asleep in Jesus.
>
> For this we say to you by the word of the Lord, that we who are alive, and remain until the coming of the Lord, shall not precede those who have fallen asleep. For the Lord Himself will descend from heaven with a shout, with the voice of the archangel, and with the trumpet of God; and the dead in Christ shall rise first.
>
> Then we who are alive and remain shall be caught up together with them in the clouds to meet the Lord in the air, and thus we shall always be with the Lord. Therefore comfort one another with these words (1 Thes. 4:13-18).

Paul also wrote to Titus about this comfort, and said that our position should be that of "looking for the blessed hope and the appearing of the glory of our great God and Saviour, Christ Jesus" (Titus 2:13). The verb tense indicates that our looking is to be constant attention. Today we could compare it to the watchfulness of a radar scanner—constant attention to the blessed hope that He is coming back for us.

Believe Completely in Christ

When Jesus said, "And you know the way where I am going," Thomas did not understand and he asked, "Lord, we do not know where You are going; how do we know the way?" (14:4-5)

Jesus responded with one of His more quoted statements: "I am the way, and the truth, and the life; no one comes to the Father, but through Me" (14:6). When your heart begins to shudder, think of this—Jesus is the way and the truth and the life. Because He spoke these words just before He went to the Cross, we can take the words as our call to the Cross. For there we find yet more comfort, not only in His saving power but also in His demonstration of love. It is this love that will see us through a troubled world.

We all experience difficulty. Sometimes life seems to nearly fall apart. But in the despair and darkness of those hours, we hear Jesus say to us, "Let not your heart be troubled; believe in God, believe also in Me."

When those troubled times come, as they will, we can discipline our minds and we can reflect on the comforting fact that we have not only a place of reward but a person of reward in our Lord Jesus Christ. And we can let Him be the healing medicine for our troubled hearts.

7
The Comforting Holy Spirit

John 14:12-27

If we truly understand the ministry of the Holy Spirit, we will find new calm in this troubled world. Jesus promised that when the Spirit would come, He would bring comfort to the hearts of believers. In the verses before us, Jesus spoke of the Holy Spirit in three aspects of His being—His nature, His ability to relate us to the Father and the Son, and His power.

A Comforting Nature

"And I will ask the Father, and He will give you another Helper, that He may be with you forever" (John 14:16). In the phrase, "another Helper," there is something significant that we need to notice. There are two Greek words which can be translated "another." One is *allos* which means "another of the same kind." The second is *heteros* which means "another of a different kind." The word Jesus used here is *allos,* meaning that the Father was to give the disciples another Helper *just like Jesus.* That was comfort! They had no cause for anxiety even though He was leaving them, because they would have the same kind of help after He left. So much the same are Christ and the Spirit that the Apostle Paul called the Holy Spirit the Spirit of Christ: "But if anyone does not have the Spirit of Christ, he does not belong to Him" (Rom. 8:9).

This promise brings comfort to us also, for each of us who truly believes in Christ has the same Comforter at all times. We don't have to wait, as with a human being, hoping that He will have a moment of time for us. Instead, we have access to Him now. He is at our side.

This Comforter, this Helper, is the Paraclete. This word often carried the meaning of a legal counsel in court, one who argues a case and stands in someone's stead. The word always contains the idea of encouragement, of one who will be there to help carry the responsibility of another.

A wonderful illustration of this comes from the experience of the Apostle Paul. When he wrote 2 Corinthians, he told the people that he had been depressed and discouraged, but that God had comforted him by the arrival of Titus. I think Titus came as a surrogate for the Holy Spirit, for Paul described his arrival this way: "But God, who comforts the depressed, comforted us by the coming of Titus" (2 Cor. 7:6). What do you think happened between Paul and Titus? I think Titus came in and said, "How are you doing, Paul, old friend? Not too well?" And then he put his arm around Paul and said, "Let's pray, Paul." After they had prayed together, I think Titus listened to Paul's concerns, and reminded him of past battles and victories. And I think they went to the Scriptures together. It wasn't long before Paul was feeling better and was again ready for action. Titus is a picture of the divine Comforter who comes alongside us to help in our times of need. The Knox translation renders *allos,* "another friend for you."

When Jesus told the disciples that another Helper was coming, He was promising one to counsel, to pick us up, to be another friend for us, to be an advocate, to be one just like Jesus. If you are going through hard times, I hope you know the reality of the comforting nature of the Holy Spirit.

A Comforting Relationship

"And I will ask the Father, and He will give you another Helper, that He may be with you forever; that is the Spirit of truth, whom the world cannot receive, because it does not behold Him or know Him, but you know Him because He abides with you, and will be in you" (14:16-17).

Not only does the Holy Spirit come alongside us, but He abides in us. In verse 23 of our text, Jesus expanded this idea in His answer to Judas the son of Alphaeus:

Jesus answered and said to him, "If anyone loves Me, he will keep My word; and My Father will love him, and We will come to him, and make Our abode with him (14:23).

Jesus was really saying that God the Father and God the Son also reside in us. This is the second time in this chapter He is referring to a special place. In the first verses of John 14 is the promise, "Let not your heart be troubled . . . for I go to prepare a place for you." The same Greek word for *place* is used in verse 2 and also in verse 23. As Jesus is preparing a dwelling place *for* us, His Spirit makes His abode *within* us.

Much of the indwelling comfort comes from the Holy Spirit being the Spirit of Truth. For this Spirit of Truth allows us to begin to understand our inner self, to make some sense of the world about us. And He brings comfort to our troubled hearts by reminding us of the Word of God:

"But the Helper, the Holy Spirit, whom the Father will send in My name, He will teach you all things, and bring to your remembrance all that I said to you" (14:26).

To the unregenerate mind, the mysteries of God's purpose in life remain barred. But to the believer, the indwelling Spirit gives comprehension and comfort. He brings before our troubled hearts the Word of God and applies its comfort. Words can never adequately convey the comfort of the Holy Spirit, but I have seen it, as I have stood in a hospital room with those whose lives are literally falling apart, and have witnessed the Holy Spirit bringing to their remembrance the promises of the Word.

"I will not leave you as orphans. I will come to you" (14:18). What Jesus was saying is, "I will not leave you fatherless." I believe this is one of the most healing of biblical truths. Although we hang our faith on the doctrine of justification, the doctrine of adoption is the one which helps us to fully draw on the other great doctrines of salvation.

I once knew a Christian who for years had had the greatest difficulty in praying to God the Father. He had always prayed to Jesus. His relationship with his own father had been very bad and he was still terribly insecure. And then he learned about the doctrine of adoption and began to make strides in his spiritual growth.

A grasp of our position as God's adopted children makes it possible for us to integrate the other Christian doctrines into our lives, and to appropriate their benefits.

> You sum up the whole of New Testament teaching in a single phrase, if you speak of it as a revelation of the Fatherhood of the holy Creator. In the same way you sum up the whole of New Testament religion if you describe it as the knowledge of God as one's holy Father. If you want to judge how well a person understands Christianity, find out how much he makes of the thought of being God's child, and having God as his Father. If this is not the thought that prompts and controls his worship and prayers and his whole outlook on life, it means that he does not understand Christianity very well at all. For everything that Christ taught, everything that makes the New Testament new, and better than the Old, everything that is distinctively Christian as opposed to merely Jewish, is summed up in the knowledge of the Fatherhood of God. 'Father' is the Christian name for God. . . . Our understanding of Christianity cannot be better than our grasp of adoption (J.I. Packer, *Knowing God,* InterVarsity Press, p. 182).

God is our Father. We have been adopted by Him. Recently a friend of mine who teaches in a seminary said that the truth of this doctrine came home to him when he saw a modern document about adoption. He told me that a natural parent can disown his children but an adoptive parent cannot. The Christian life can be understood only in terms of the security of adoption. As God loved His only begotten Son, Jesus, so He loves His adopted children. As God has fellowship with Jesus, so He has fellowship with us, by virtue of our adoption. As God has exalted the Lord Jesus, so He will exalt us, as joint heirs with Christ.

"For the Father Himself loves you, because you have loved Me, and have believed that I came forth from the Father" (16:27).

What we have seen and heard we proclaim to you also, that you also may have fellowship with us; and indeed our fellowship is with the Father, and with His Son Jesus Christ (1 John 1:3).

Beloved, now we are children of God, and it has not appeared as yet what we shall be. We know that, if He should appear, we shall be like Him, because we shall see Him just as He is (1 John 3:2).

The words, "I will not leave you as orphans, but will come to you," speak of how the Spirit reminds us of the reality of our adoption. He keeps us aware that we are God's children, even in times when we try to deny it. And in this awareness He gives us faith and joy. Also, He prompts us to look to God as Father with the perfect trust that is natural to secure children. He intensifies within us that "spirit of adoption" which makes us cry, "Abba, Father" or "Dearest Father." (See Romans 8:15 and Galatians 4:6.) And He moves us toward a way of life commensurate with our royal position as children of God, by developing a family likeness.

A Comforting Power

"Truly, truly, I say to you, he who believes in Me, the works that I do shall he do also; and greater works than these shall he do; because I go to the Father" (14:12).

Because the Holy Spirit indwells us, we do the same works as Jesus—and they are greater than His works, simply because of the humble weakness of His instruments. An incident which comes to us from World War II beautifully portrays this truth. During the war in the Pacific, a sailor on a United States submarine was stricken with acute appendicitis. The nearest surgeon was thousands of miles away. Pharmacist Mate Wheller Lipes watched the seaman's temperature rise to 106 degrees. His only hope was an operation. Said Lipes: "I have watched doctors do it. I think I could. What do you say?" The sailor consented.

In the wardroom, about the size of a pullman drawing room, the patient was stretched out on a table beneath a floodlight. The mate and assisting officers, dressed in reversed pajama tops, masked their faces with gauze. The crew stood by the diving planes to keep the ship steady; the cook boiled water for sterilizing. A tea strainer served as an antiseptic cone. A broken-handled scalpel was the operating instrument. Alcohol drained from the torpedoes was the antiseptic. Bent tablespoons served to keep the muscles open. After cutting through the layers of muscle, the mate took twenty minutes to find the appendix. Two and a half hours later, the last catgut stitch was sewed, just as the last drop of ether gave out. Thirteen days later the patient was back at work (*Let Me Illustrate,* Barnhouse, Fleming H. Revell, pp. 358-359).

Lipes' work was greater than the work of a surgeon, not because it was better, but because it was performed by a humble sailor. So it is with us, the same power that through Jesus brought regeneration and life to people of His day flows through us despite our weakness. In that sense, our work is greater. The same wisdom that brought healing to the most fragmented relationships is operable in us. The same miraculous love that brought life to impossible situations resides in us.

"Peace I leave with you; My peace I give to you; not as the world gives, do I give to you. Let not your heart be troubled, nor let it be fearful" (14:27).

The same peace that Jesus had is our peace. This is the remedy for troubled hearts. Not only is there a future place for us, but there is a place now in which Jesus gives us a Comforter just like Himself, a family likeness to Himself through our adoption, and the power to do His works in the world.

8
On Bearing Fruit
John 15:1-11

As Jesus continued to talk with His disciples in the Upper Room, He may have looked out of the window and seen the moonlit tendrils of a grapevine, because He began to speak to them of vines and branches. This had deep symbolic value to them, for Israel was thought of as the vine. In Isaiah 5:7 we read, "For the vineyard of the Lord of hosts is the house of Israel, and the men of Judah His delightful plant."

The grapevine was the symbol of their national life. It was the emblem on coins minted during the Maccabbean period. So precious was the vine as a symbol that a huge gold grapevine decorated the gates of the Temple.

In the Temple at Jerusalem, above and round the gate, seventy cubits high, which led from the porch to the holy place, a richly carved vine was extended as a border and decoration. The branches, tendrils, and leaves were of finest gold; the stalks of the bunches were of the length of the human form, and the bunches hanging upon them were of costly jewels. Herod first placed it there; rich and patriotic Jews from time to time added to its embellishment, one contributed a new grape, another a leaf, and a third even a bunch of the same precious materials . . . this vine must have had an uncommon importance and a sacred meaning in the eyes of the Jews. With what majestic splendor must it likewise have appeared in the evening, when it was illuminated by tapers! (*Calmet's Dictionary of the Holy Bible,* Charles Taylor, p. 877).

For His seventh and final "I Am" statement, Jesus said, "I am the true Vine, and My Father is the Vinedresser" (John 15:1). His statement would have drawn together all the history of the vine as a national symbol. It was as if He were saying, "You know how Israel is pictured as a vine which is to produce refreshing fruit. Well, I am the authentic Vine, the fulfillment of all that this symbol suggests."

For us as Christian believers, His statement is a wonderfully deep and mystic parable. Christ is the Vine (the trunk of the tree), we are the branches, and God is the Gardener. The picture is of believers organically related to Christ. The sap that runs in the veins of the Vine runs also in the veins of the branches. The Gardener walks among the vines lovingly caring for them so that they might bring forth fruit.

The overriding emphasis of the passage is fruit-bearing.

"Every branch in Me that does not bear fruit, He takes away; and every branch that bears fruit, He prunes it, that it may bear more fruit (15:2).

"Abide in Me, and I in you. As the branch cannot bear fruit of itself, unless it abides in the vine, so neither can you, unless you abide in Me (15:4).

"I am the vine, you are the branches; he who abides in Me, and I in him, he bears much fruit; for apart from Me you can do nothing (15:5).

"By this is My Father glorified, that you bear much fruit, and so prove to be My disciples" (15:8).

Fruit-bearing is the identifying mark of the true believer. "Every branch in Me that does not bear fruit, He takes away." Some people claim to be in the Vine, but the absence of fruit disqualifies them. On another occasion Jesus had said, "You will know them by their fruits" (Matt. 7:20). Jesus is teaching us that if there is no fruit, we had better reconsider the authenticity of our Christianity.

God Looks for Fruit

"I am the true Vine, and My Father is the Vinedresser. Every branch in Me that does not bear fruit, He takes away; and every branch that bears fruit, He prunes it, that it may bear more fruit" (15:1-2).

A preacher received a letter from a girl who was in a state of spiritual distress. She had never won anyone to Christ, and felt that she had not been fruitful in her spiritual life. While this kind of reproduction is very important, it is not what Jesus had in mind in these verses. A passage from Isaiah tells us what He meant:

Let me sing now for my well-beloved a song of my beloved concerning his vineyard. My well-beloved had a vineyard on a fertile hill. And he dug it all around, removed its stones, and planted it with the choicest vine. And he built a tower in the middle of it, and hewed out a wine vat in it; then he expected it to produce good grapes, but it produced only worthless ones (Isa. 5:1-2).

Those worthless grapes that Israel produced—what were they like? Isaiah 5:7 tells us: "Thus He looked for justice, but behold, bloodshed; for righteousness, but behold, a cry of distress." The fruit He was looking for was in the qualities of justice and righteousness, qualities which are intrinsically inward.

The fruit of which Jesus was speaking is the reproduction of the life of the Vine in the branches. Jesus looks for His life in us. If the inward graces of the Holy Spirit are not present in our lives, the love, joy, peace, patience, kindness, goodness, faithfulness, gentleness, self-control, if these qualities are not working in our lives—we must grapple with the possibility that we may not be true believers.

I believe this inward test is far more telling than the number of souls saved, people influenced, money collected, etc. It is possible to have the outward signs without having the life of Christ within. Yet when the inward graces of the Spirit are present, they normally produce the outward signs. The fruit Christ looks for is His own life in us.

God Prunes for Fruit

"Every branch that bears fruit, He prunes it, that it may bear more fruit" (15:2). The branches which are doing well, which best convey the life of the vine, get the knife. If you have ever driven through a vineyard, you know what I mean. During the winter all you see are bare twisted trunks. But in the summer you see endless rows of lush green grapevines expanding their foliage so fast you can almost see them growing. Their health is directly proportionate to their pruning.

Grape-growers, viticulturalists as they call themselves, practice four stages of pruning. First, there is pinching to remove the growing tip so that it will not grow too rapidly. Then there is topping, when a foot or two of new growth will be removed to prevent the loss of an entire shoot. Thinning the grape clusters enables the rest of a branch to bear more and better fruit. Finally, there is the cutting away of suckers, to give more nourishment to the whole vine. In the fall and winter, the vines are pruned so that the main stock will produce a better yield the following year (James E. Rosscup, *Abiding in Christ*, Zondervan, p. 50).

This is a drastic process and to the uninitiated it looks wasteful. But to the experienced grower, it is the only means of producing healthy, delicious fruit.

What is involved in pruning? Pain. Pruning always hurts. King David said, "Before I was afflicted I went astray" (Ps. 119:67). And again, "It is good for me that I was afflicted" (Ps. 119:71). Sometimes the pain of pruning comes because of our sins. Other times, it is simply because we are bearing abundant fruit and God wants us to bear more. Whatever the reason, it is always something that our natural selves want to escape. No one wants the knife. And yet true Christians must know that it will never stop.

Sometimes Christians are subject to the When Syndrome. "When I become spiritually mature, these things won't happen to me." "When I get married, things will change." "When I retire, I won't have these painful experiences."

The affliction of pruning is stopped only when it is useless. Therefore, the true Christian knows that it will continue, for it is good for us. In *Jesus Rediscovered,* Malcolm Muggeridge speaks about pain:

> Suppose you eliminated suffering, what a dreadful place the world would be. I would almost rather eliminate happiness. The world would be the most ghastly place because everything that corrects the tendency of this unspeakable little creature, man, to feel over-important and over-pleased with himself would disappear. He's bad enough now, but he would be absolutely intolerable if he never suffered (Collins, Glasgow: 1976, p. 188).

Some years ago I set off on a grandiose spiritual scheme. I shared the idea with my friends and they told me it was great and assured me that it would succeed. I had good motives and the ideas were sound. Yet, to my great embarrassment, I fell flat on my face. As I talked over my failure with a close friend, he said, "You know what? This is good for you. If you had succeeded at this, you would have started going to other churches, telling others how to do it. Then you might have begun giving seminars. This is the best thing that could have happened."

Eustace Scrubb is a boy who thinks only about himself. In C.S. Lewis' *The Voyage of the Dawn Treader,* he finds himself in a dragon's cave. Suddenly, he discovers that he has turned into a dragon. Naturally, he attempts to take off his dragon skin, but he can't remove it by himself. Finally, the lion, the Christ figure, comes to him, and as Eustace relates it:

"Then the lion said—but I don't know if it spoke—'You will have to let me undress you.' I was afraid of his claws, I can tell you, but I was pretty nearly desperate now. So I just lay flat down on my back to let him do it.

"The very first tear he made was so deep that I thought it had gone right into my heart. And when he began pulling the skin off, it hurt worse than anything I've ever felt. The only thing that made me able to bear it was just the pleasure of feeling the stuff peel off" (London: Collins, 1974, p. 102).

What is noble and attractive in our lives is the result of the cutting and pain which we would have avoided if we could have. We looked at King David's words about affliction. In the second half of each of the two verses, he tells the result of the affliction in his life:

Before I was afflicted, I went astray, but now I keep Thy Word. . . .
It is good for me that I was afflicted, that I may learn Thy statutes (Ps. 119: 67, 71).

James, the half brother of our Lord, learned this truth and wrote to the early church:

Dear brothers, is your life full of difficulties and temptations? Then be happy, for when the way is rough, your patience has a chance to grow. So let it grow, and don't try to squirm out of your problems. For when your patience is finally in full bloom, then you will be ready for anything, strong in character, full and complete (James 1:2, TLB).

Something else about this matter of pruning—Christ's hand is never closer to us than when He prunes in our lives. During times of severest cutting, when we may feel that He is all but gone, He is really the closest. We need to remember that while pruning may pain us, it will never harm us. When a gardener prunes, he leaves little more than the vine. In our lives, the more we are pruned, the more proportionately of Christ there is in our experience. And when the branch bears fruit, it is not for itself but for others. The life that has borne trimming by the hand of God is the life that sustains other people.

The Gardener prunes that we might bear fruit, but that is not all. When we do bear fruit, He prunes that we might bear more fruit: "Every branch that bears fruit, He prunes it, that it may bear more fruit" (15:2). The more productive our lives are, the more they will be trimmed. The poet and hymn writer John Newton expressed the idea this way:

> I asked the Lord, that I might grow
>   In faith, and love, and every grace;
> Might more of His salvation know,
>   And seek more earnestly His face.
>
> I hoped that in some favoured hour
>   At once He'd answer my request,
> And by His love's constraining power
>   Subdue my sins, and give me rest.
>
> Instead of this, He made me feel
>   The hidden evils of my heart;
> And let the angry powers of hell
>   Assault my soul in every part.
>
> Yea more, with His own hand He seemed
>   Intent to aggravate my woe;
> Crossed all the fair designs I schemed,
>   Blasted my gourds, and laid me low.
>
> "Lord, why is this?" I trembling cried,
>   "Wilt thou pursue Thy worm to death?"
> "Tis in this way," the Lord replied,
>   "I answer prayer for grace and faith.
>
> "These inward trials I employ
>   From self and pride to set thee free;
> And break thy schemes of earthly joy,
>   That thou may'st seek thy all in Me."

God's Condition for Fruit

"Abide in Me, and I in you. As the branch cannot bear fruit of itself, unless it abides in the vine, so neither can you, unless you abide in Me. I am the Vine, you are the branches; he who abides in Me, and I in him, he bears much fruit; for apart from Me you can do nothing" (15:4-5).

What does it mean to abide? I personally believe that the sap which runs between the Vine and the branches is suggestive of the Holy Spirit, and that abiding is parallel to being filled with the Holy Spirit. When we abide, we set aside everything else from which we might derive strength and merit, to draw all from Christ.

Our text says that without Christ we can do nothing. And yet there are many things we can do without Christ. We can earn a living, raise a family, and practice generosity. It is possible to pastor a church without abiding in Christ. It is possible to counsel people without abiding. Our generation understands this—people today think they can do nearly everything by themselves.

What does Christ mean that apart from Him we can do nothing? He means that without Him we cannot bear spiritual fruit. We could tie fruit on the vine, like ornaments on a Christmas tree, but it would not be real. Real fruit comes from the character and life of the vine. However, before we can abide we have to personally believe that we can't do anything of spiritual worth without Him.

One reason for frequent pruning is that we are brought back to this dependence on God. God does not shield us from the assaults of life, but rather exposes us, to ensure that we will learn to hold fast to Him. Abiding involves a growing sense of our own weakness. Jesus expressed this in the first Beatitude: "Blessed are the poor in spirit, for theirs is the kingdom of heaven" (Matt. 5:3).

Those who learn well to abide will stay put for the pruning. We need the will to abide, the will to get into the Word, the will to associate with other believers, the will to put ourselves into places where we can grow.

> "If you abide in Me, and My words abide in you, ask whatever you wish, and it shall be done for you. By this is My Father glorified, that you bear much fruit, and so prove to be My disciples" (15:7-8).

As we pray, we abide. As we abide, we pray more, and more deeply. And God is glorified by what is happening in our lives.

> "Just as the Father has loved Me, I have also loved you; abide in My love. If you keep My commandments, you will abide in My love; just as I have kept My Father's commandments, and abide in His love. These things I have spoken to you, that My joy may be in you, and that your joy may be made full" (15:9-11).

Our lives are filled with love and with joy. G.K. Chesterton called this joy "the gigantic secret of the Christian" (*Orthodoxy*, New York: Lane, 1909, p. 160). And in the life of abiding, joy reaches its maximum and then keeps on increasing.

9
Loving the Branches
John 15:12-17

John R. Claypool, in *The Preaching Event,* tells this story about identical twin boys:

The boys' lives became inseparably intertwined. From the first they dressed alike, went to the same schools, did all the same things. In fact, they were so close that neither ever married, but they came back and took over the running of the family business when their father died. Their relationship to each other was pointed to as a model of creative collaboration.

One morning a customer came into the store and made a small purchase. The brother who waited on him put the dollar bill on top of the cash register and walked to the front door with the man. Some time later he remembered what he had done, but when he went to the cash register, he found the dollar gone. He asked his brother if he had seen the bill and put it into the register, and the brother replied that he knew nothing of the bill.

"That's funny," said the other, "I distinctly remember placing the bill here on the register, and no one else has been in the store since then."

Had the matter been dropped at that point—a mystery involving a tiny amount of money—nothing would have come of it. However, an hour later, this time with a noticeable hint of suspicion in his voice, the brother asked again, "Are you sure you didn't see that dollar bill and put it into the register?" The other brother was quick to catch the note of accusation, and flare back in defensive anger.

This was the beginning of the first serious breach of trust that had ever come between these two. It grew wider and wider. Every time they tried to discuss the issue, new charges and countercharges got mixed into the brew, until finally things got so bad that they were forced to dissolve their partnership. They ran a partition down the middle of their father's store and turned what had once been a harmonious partnership into an angry competition. In fact, that business became a source of division in the whole community, each twin trying to enlist allies for himself against the other. This warfare went on for more than twenty years.

Then one day a car with an out-of-state license parked in front of the store. A well-dressed man got out, went into one of the sides, and inquired how long the merchant had been in business in that location. When he found it was more than twenty years, the stranger said, "Then you are the one with whom I must settle an old score."

"Some twenty years ago," he said, "I was out of work, drifting from place to place, and I happened to get off a box car in your town. I had absolutely no money and had not eaten for three days. As I was walking down the alley behind your store, I looked in and saw a dollar bill on the top of the cash register. Everyone else was in the front of the store. I had been raised in a Christian home and I had never before in all my life stolen anything, but that morning I was so hungry, I gave in to the temptation, slipped through the door and took that dollar bill. That act has weighed on my conscience ever since, and I finally decided that I would never be at peace until I came back and faced up to that old sin and made amends. Would you let me now replace that money and pay you whatever is appropriate for damages?"

At that point the stranger was surprised to see the old man shaking his head in dismay and beginning to weep. When the brother had gotten control of himself, he took the stranger by the arm and said, "I want you to go next door, and repeat the same story you have just told me." The stranger did, only this time there were two old men, who looked remarkably alike, both weeping uncontrollably (Word Books, pp. 37-40).

This story, and our recollections of others like it, bring into sharp focus the friendship and love that should exist between Christian brothers and sisters. All of John 15 is concerned with the believer's relationships. In verses 1-11 we see the relationship between the Vine and the branches, or Christ and believers. Now, in verses 12-17, we see the relationship of branch to branch, or believer to believer. Verses 18-27 deal with the relationship of the Vine and branches to the world.

One reason we keenly feel the need for friendship and love between believers is that so many in the body of Christ are lonely and anxious for friendship. Craig W. Ellison writes:

Loneliness seems to have flooded the lives of millions of modern Americans. It's an emotional epidemic. A recent survey of over 40,000 respondents of all ages found that 67 percent of them felt lonely some of the time. Projected nationally, that amounts to over 150 million Americans who have personally experienced loneliness. Another survey found that over 64 percent of widows over age 50 in several major urban areas mentioned loneliness as a significant problem in their lives. United Methodist men have established a nationwide 24-hour, toll-free telephone line for people wanting to pray with someone. Loneliness is the most frequently mentioned prayer need that they receive. Contact, a nationwide crisis intervention telephone network, received over 18,000 calls due to intense loneliness in one recent six-month period (*Loneliness: the Search for Intimacy.* Christian Herald Books, p. 17).

There are Christians who would give almost anything for one good friend. The principles in our text govern the initiation, the reception, and the maintenance of friendship. And as the friendship develops, these principles take us into yet deeper relationships.

Sacrifice

"This is My commandment, that you love one another, just as I have loved you. Greater love has no one than this, that one lay down his life for his friends" (15:12-13).

These verses are a restatement of the new commandment given in John 13:34: "A new commandment I give to you, that you love one another, even as I have loved you, that you also love one another." The idea of sacrifice is found in the phrase, "As I have loved you." The old commandment was to love God with everything in us, and our neighbors as ourselves. The story of the Good Samaritan was Christ's great explanation of that kind of love, and it was a wonderful love indeed. But the new commandment requires us to love as Jesus loved. His sacrifice is to be our model. Jesus calls for sacrificial love in His church, extended from branch to branch.

Our Lord illustrated this. Just before He gave the new commandment, He had tried in every way to restore Judas with sacrificial love. Now Christ was translating His actions into words, thus officially making sacrifice an essential characteristic of love between believers. True friendship has recurring sacrifice as its base.

A story from the life of E. Stanley Jones gives a beautiful example of this sacrificial principle. It occurred when he was preaching his first evangelistic service among some poor mountaineers of Kentucky. The meetings were being held in the schoolhouse. After the first meeting at the schoolhouse:

> I was invited to stay with a man and wife, and when I arrived I saw there was one bed. The husband said, "You take the far side." Then he got in, and then his wife. In the morning we reversed the process. I turned my face to the wall as they dressed, and then they stepped out while I dressed. That was real hospitality! I have slept in palaces, but the hospitality of that one-bed home is the most memorable and the most appreciated (E. Stanley Jones, *A Song of Ascents,* Abingdon, pp. 129-30).

Dr. Jones felt a lifelong affection for that humble couple who demonstrated so poignantly the sacrificial principle. Often people who are without friends come up short here. Because of unsuccessful relationships, they have withdrawn, waiting for someone to do something for them. Or, perhaps they do a kind act for someone else, but that person doesn't respond, so they withdraw. The withdrawal is not seen by others for what it is, but is viewed as unfriendliness, even hostility.

Being a friend means being a giver. Friendship thrives on sacrifice. There isn't enough of this in God's family. The befriended and the friendless all need to heed this. Those with friends must consciously cultivate a sacrificial spirit and constantly work at being givers. Those without friends must do the same, for sacrifice is a primary principle of friendship.

Mutuality

Jesus' words, "You are My friends, if you do what I command you" (15:14), speak primarily of obedience, but they also suggest a mutuality of heart. Jesus' friends obey Him because they share the same outlook and goals. Close friends agree in heart. They may disagree but their hearts' aims are the same. In this respect, the Apostle Paul used a very enlightening phrase in Philippians 2:19-20:

> But I hope in the Lord Jesus to send Timothy to you shortly, so that I also may be encouraged when I learn of your condition. For I have no one else of kindred spirit who will genuinely be concerned for your welfare.

Paul described Timothy as being "of kindred spirit," meaning literally "one-souled." We think *soul brothers* is a pop term that began in the 1960s. Actually it is 2,000 years old. Because Paul and Timothy's friendship was a soul friendship, because there was a mutuality of heart, they didn't have to explain everything.

Mutuality of heart was the basis of David and Jonathan's relationship. First Samuel records its dramatic beginning, after David had killed Goliath:

> Now it came about when he had finished speaking to Saul, that the soul of Jonathan was knit to the soul of David, and Jonathan loved him as himself (1 Sam. 18:1).

Their friendship was a story of mutuality of heart and their souls were knit together. This is the type of relationship that should exist between husband and wife. Yet friendship is not exclusive to one person. The ideal is to have several who are your soul brothers and sisters, with whom you can share and be one.

This mutuality of heart is ennobled and promoted by the sharing of personal information:

> "No longer do I call you slaves; for the slave does not know what his master is doing; but I have called you friends, for all things that I have heard from My Father I have made known to you" (15:15).

Jesus shared the deepest thoughts of His heart with His men. This fostered their mutuality. In the culture of that day, slaves were considered little more than objects. Even Aristotle put slaves on the same level as inanimate objects—agricultural implements. In Jesus' day, masters did not share with their slaves, just as today most employers do not share their deepest thoughts with their employees. Yet, in genuine friendship, there are no spiritual barriers.

We need friendships that reach to the soul. We need close friends who can objectify our thoughts. We need the healing that comes when we reveal our feelings to another, without fear that our confidence will be broken. Confidential encounters among the branches can be healing.

Promotion

> "You did not choose Me, but I chose you, and appointed you, that you should go and bear fruit, and that your fruit should remain; that whatever you ask of the Father in My name, He may give to you" (15:16).

In this verse, we see our Lord's desire to help His friends. He was committed to their fulfilling the ultimate in their calling. When you have a friend, you rejoice in his success.

Let's look again at the friendship of David and Jonathan. Just following the verse we already read are these:

> Then Jonathan made a covenant with David because he loved him as himself. And Jonathan stripped himself of the robe that was on him and gave it to David, with his armor, including his sword and his bow and his belt (1 Sam. 18:3-4).

Jonathan gave David the items that represented his station in life. As the son of the king and heir to the throne, he committed himself to make the Lord's anointed one, David, the king. In the same way but with greater intensity, Jesus is committed to the fulfillment of all that He sees we can become. And we too are to be committed to the ultimate fulfillment of our friends, even to making them live as kings.

Some time ago, our pastoral staff realized that we needed to spend more time together. Now, each week we sit down together and talk about our personal needs and goals, and then pray for and encourage one another. Often in discussing our relationships, we have said that we want to make one another as kings, to confer the royalty that a loving and supporting friendship can mutually convey.

We don't always feel like kings. In fact, most people rarely feel that way. There are so many in the body of Christ who never reach their potential because no one ever encourages them. There are some who would reach unimaginable heights if only someone would see what they could be and then urge them in that direction. But no one prays for them, befriends them, promotes them. As Christ's friends, we are called to this encouraging work of mutual promotion.

These three principles of relationship for the members of the body of Christ are not optional. Jesus' words to His disciples, and to us, are framed by two verses that use the word *command:*

> "This is My commandment, that you love one another, just as I have loved you."

"This I command you, that you love one another" (15:12, 17).

While the love of Christ is unnatural to us, it is still possible. The potential for the *agape* love which our Lord commands exists within the relationship of abiding in Him. As we as branches abide in the Vine, we will relate in right fashion to the other branches. We will sacrifice for each other. We will foster a deep mutuality, and we will promote one another until we all feel like kings.

10
If the World Hates You . . .
John 15:18—16:4

In June 1926, John Roots, a young correspondent recently grad-
uated from Harvard, was in China. In the course of his work,
he sought an interview with a shadowy Bolshevik figure, Michael Borodin, who had been the cause of considerable chaos
in Western trade. The young reporter traveled to Canton, pre-
sented his credentials to Borodin's secretary—who was later
known to the world as Ho Chi Minh—and was ushered into the
Russian's presence.

> I found my hand being pumped by a burly six-footer clad in a
> crumpled white jacket and trousers, with a shock of unruly black
> hair, a neat handlebar mustache, and a booming voice that bade
> strangers welcome in heavily accented but fluent and idiomatic
> American English (John McCook Roots, *Chou: An Informal Biog-
> raphy of China's Legendary Chou En-Lai,* Doubleday, p. 32).

As they sat down to visit, Roots' mind sped through the scant
information available about Borodin. He had been handpicked
by Lenin for his present job. Earlier he had taught school in
Indiana and had served time in a Glasgow jail.

The reporter eagerly began the interview, asking questions
about the realism of Borodin's goals. But shortly, the tables
were turned as Borodin pressed the attack:

You forget, young man, that I am not here for my health, or I would not be working in this barbarous heat. I don't spend my time at the bars and the races like the English and French. I am not interested in a career or a fortune like the Americans. I serve an ideology. And with an ideology it is not numbers that count. It is dedication. You Americans would not understand that. I have lived many years in your country and I know what goes on. You concentrate on comfort and personal success" (Roots, *Chou,* pp. 33-34).

As Borodin continued his attack, Roots tried to regain control of the interview as he asked: "Do you enjoy your work in China, Mr. Borodin?"

"Enjoy!" he echoed scornfully. "A bourgeois question. It is not a matter of whether we enjoy our work here. The work is necessary. That is all that counts. It is, of course, far from the friends, the concerts, and the theater that mean so much in Moscow. But long ago I made up my mind that Communism alone held an answer for the world. . . . Nothing else matters. Does that answer your question?" (Roots, *Chou,* p. 34)

The pursuit of enjoyment is an American preoccupation, more American today than it was fifty years ago or even twenty years ago. Our culture's commitments are largely determined by the question of personal enjoyment. Within proper perspective, enjoyment is important, but today it has become a controlling force in American life.

It is no accident that at the present time the dominant trend in psychoanalysis is the rediscovery of narcissism.

Our society is marked by a self-interest and egocentrism that increasingly reduces all relations to the question, "What am I getting out of it?"

The pursuit of enjoyment has penetrated the church. There is a growing belief that Christianity is to make us healthy and wealthy and problem-free.

Now it is true that a healthy spiritual life does contribute to physical health. And it is also true that attention to spiritual principles often aids our prosperity. But not necessarily.

Godly believers are not always wealthy. Godly believers sometimes have physical difficulties. Sometimes they suffer injus-
tices or are persecuted. The danger of the health-wealth-
happiness expectation is obvious. When life doesn't fit our theological box, we tend to toss the whole thing over. Or we may
deny the reality of our situation.

What Should the Christian Expect?
What are proper expectations for the Christian as he follows
Christ in a sinful world?

> "If the world hates you, you know that it has hated Me before
> it hated you. If you were of the world, the world would love its
> own; but because you are not of the world, but I chose you out
> of the world, therefore the world hates you. Remember the
> word that I said to you, 'A slave is not greater than his master.'
> If they persecuted Me, they will also persecute you; if they kept
> My word, they will keep yours also" (John 15:18-20).

These words must have jolted Christ's disciples, since He had
just been speaking words of hope and peace and love and fruit-
fulness in service. This message was certainly not one of
enjoyment.

The Greek suggests certainty—you *will be* hated. Jesus offered
several reasons for this reaction. The world hated Jesus, and
without cause.

> "If I had not come and spoken to them, they would not have sin,
> but now they have no excuse for their sin. He who hates Me
> hates My Father also. If I had not done among them the works
> which no one else did, they would not have sin; but now they
> have both seen and hated Me and My Father as well. But
> they have done this in order that the word may be fulfilled
> that is written in their Law, 'They hated Me without a cause' "
> (15:22-25).

Both His works and His words provided a startling contrast
to the lives of the people, and they hated Him for that. His inner

righteousness earned their abiding hostility because it revealed the shabbiness of their external religiosity.

Many years ago, a certain African chief paid a visit to a mission station. Hanging on a tree outside the missionary's cabin was a little mirror. The chief, who by the way was a woman, looked into the mirror and saw her reflection with its war paint and menacing features. She gazed at her own terrifying likeness and then turned in horror toward the missionary: "Who is that horrible looking person inside your tree?"

"Oh," the missionary answered, "it is not in the tree. The glass is showing you your own face." The chief would not believe until she held the mirror in her hands.

Then she said, "I must have this glass. How much will you sell it for?"

"I don't want to sell it," said the missionary. But wanting to please the chief, he named a price and took the mirror down from the tree. As he handed it to the chief, she threw it on the ground, exclaiming, "I will never again have that making faces at me!"

Jesus was a mirror to people of their own lives in contrast to His, and it was too much for them, so they sought to break the mirror. The same thing happens today—a good look at Jesus is more than some people can handle, and they react with hatred. A loyal follower of Christ who mirrors his Lord must expect this reaction. We are not of this world:

"If you were of the world, the world would love its own; but because you are not of the world, but I chose you out of the world, therefore the world hates you" (15:19).

The word for world used five times in verse 19 is *kosmos* which refers to the sinful world system. In other words, the world hates you because you are not part of its system. It always opposes those who do not conform.

But it would be a mistake to think that persecution is always violent, that the godly Christian is constantly persecuted, or that every unbeliever hates Christians. The system always does, but not every individual in that system.

When persecution occurs, it can wear many faces. Most often it is shown in attitude, sometimes an indifference that treats Christians as nonentities. Other times it is avoidance, as antagonists reroute their paths or reschedule their breaks. Occasionally, it reaches growing animosity or repulsion.

The word for persecute in verse 20 means "to chase like a wild beast." While we don't experience this violence here, it is happening in many parts of the world. The recently martyred missionary, Chet Bitterman, knew it.

There have been more martyrs for Christ in the twentieth century than in any other century. The physical suffering of the early church is being reenacted every day. It could happen here. And if it does, it will affect the health and wealth of believers, notwithstanding the mouthings of those who say, "I will live in divine health," or "God wants me rich." The world persecutes those who are not part of the system.

What is true for the greater is also true for the lesser. Jesus said, "If they persecuted Me, they will also persecute you" (15:20). And when this happens, persecution is proportionate to the extent of a person's identification with Christ. Pastor Dietrich Bonhoeffer was executed at the end of World War II in a German concentration camp. In 1937 he wrote these words:

> Suffering . . . is the badge of true discipleship. The disciple is not above his master. . . . Luther reckoned suffering among the marks of the true church. . . . Discipleship means allegiance to the suffering Christ, and it is therefore not at all surprising that Christians should be called upon to suffer (*The Cost of Discipleship*, Macmillan, pp. 100-101).

How Does the Christian View Persecution?

Jesus' teaching demands that we draw some conclusions about the matter of persecution. Smooth sailing is not necessarily a sign that God is pleased with our lives. The absence of persecution may actually indicate that something is wrong. Such was the case with Lot. He had become tired of the separated life in the hills of Palestine and moved his tents ever nearer to Sodom until he was firmly entrenched in the life of the wicked city. Life went along very well for Lot because he followed Sodom's systems. He was so much a part of it that in the end when he told his family that the angels had revealed that judgment was coming, "He appeared to his sons-in-law to be jesting" (Gen. 19:14). Lot was too comfortable in Sodom.

Most people we know are not as crass as Lot, but they do try to find a comfortable spot between the extremes of a godly life and sinful life. They prefer smooth sailing to being possessed by God, and this is why they go through life with so little difficulty. They have accommodated themselves to the world—at the cost of their souls.

On the other side, we need to remember that persecution is not necessarily a sign of God's approval. The godly aren't always under the sword. In Proverbs 16:7 we read: "When a man's ways are pleasing to the Lord, he makes even his enemies to be at peace with him." Quite frankly, some believers are persecuted because of their own stupidity or rudeness or annoying personalities or false piety.

God is pleased with a life that demonstrates the righteousness of Christ in both words and actions. Daniel is the only major person in the Bible of whom no sin is recorded. He was an exemplary man, so faultless that the world system tried to kill him by throwing him into a den of lions. But God stopped the lions' mouths.

William Temple's words could apply to Daniel and to all who live truly godly lives:

The world ... would not hate angels for being angelic; but it does hate men for being Christians. It grudges them their new character; it is tormented by their peace; it is infuriated by their joy (William Temple, *Readings in John's Gospel,* London: Macmillan, 1945, p. 272).

The Apostles Paul and Peter wrote to first-century Christians about the afflictions they were or could expect to suffer.

And indeed, all who desire to live godly in Christ Jesus will be persecuted (2 Tim. 3:12).

For to you it has been granted for Christ's sake, not only to believe in Him, but also to suffer for His sake (Phil. 1:29).

. . .so that no man may be disturbed by these afflictions; for you yourselves know that we have been destined for this (1 Thes. 3:3).

Beloved, do not be surprised at the fiery ordeal among you, which comes upon you for your testing, as though some strange thing were happening to you; but to the degree that you share the sufferings of Christ, keep on rejoicing (1 Peter 4:12-13).

What Does God Expect of Christians?

When persecution comes to us, what are we to do? Draw back? Retaliate? Seek revenge? No! We are forbidden to return evil for evil. What then does God expect of us?

Persecution is not an excuse for silence, but a challenge to witness. We are to share Christ lovingly to a hostile world, in the power of the Holy Spirit, just as our text tells us:

"When the Helper comes, whom I will send to you from the Father, that is, the Spirit of truth, who proceeds from the Father, He will bear witness of Me, and you will bear witness also, because you have been with Me from the beginning" (15:26-27).

A beautiful Valentine story illustrates the quality of this witness. Little Stevie who was quiet and shy had just moved with his family to a new neighborhood. One day he came home from school and said to his mom, "You know what? Valentine's Day is coming and I want to make a card for everyone in my class. I want them all to know that I love them."

His mother's heart sank as she thought, "I wish he wouldn't do that." Every afternoon she had watched the children walking home from school, laughing and hanging on to each other—all except Stevie, that is. He always walked behind them. But because he was so determined, she decided to help him, and bought everything he would need.

For two weeks, Stevie painstakingly made valentines, thirty-five of them. When the great day came to deliver them, he was so excited. This was his day. He stashed those valentines under his arm and ran out the door. His mother watched him go and thought, "This is going to be a tough day for Stevie. I'll bake some cookies for when he comes home from school. Maybe that will ease the pain, since he won't be getting many valentines."

That afternoon she had the warm cookies and a glass of milk on the kitchen table ready for him. She went to the window to watch the children on their way home. Sure enough, there came a big gang of boys, laughing, and with valentines tucked under their arms. And there was her Stevie. Although he was behind the children, he was walking faster than usual, and she thought, "Bless his heart. He's ready to break into tears." His hands were empty—he didn't have even one valentine.

When Stevie came into the house, his mother said, "Sweetheart, Mom has some warm cookies and some milk for you. Just sit down. . . ." But Stevie's face was all aglow. He marched right by her and exclaimed: "Not a one. Not a single one! I didn't forget one. They all know I love them!"

Our Lord Jesus didn't get any "valentines" either, rather persecution. But He responded by giving His heart; and He didn't miss one—not a single one. That was Jesus' response to persecution. It is to be ours also.

As Jesus continued talking with His disciples, He got even more specific about the kind of persecution they could expect, and the reasons He was telling them all of this:

> "These things I have spoken to you, that you may be kept from stumbling. They will make you outcasts from the synagogue; but an hour is coming for everyone who kills you to think that he is offering service to God. And these things they will do, because they have not known the Father, or Me. But these things I have spoken to you, that when their hour comes, you may remember that I told you of them" (16:1-4).

"I have told you all of this so that you will not be disillusioned, assuming that you were to have smooth sailing because you were following Me. And so that you will not stumble over the theological box of narcissism and comfort."

What Jesus prophesied came true; the disciples did not stumble. It is thought that all but John died as martyrs. They understood that as Jesus was hated, so were they; for they were not part of the world order. With love and great courage, they had maintained their witness for Christ, paying the ultimate price of discipleship.

During John Roots' years as a foreign correspondent in China, he saw Michael Borodin one other time. Borodin was in a more contemplative mood than usual, and in the course of the conversation, they discussed Christianity:

> After a long silence, Borodin, still gazing out the window, began murmuring, half to himself. "You know," he mused, "I used to read the New Testament. Again and again I read it. It is the most wonderful story ever told. That man Paul. He was a *real* revolutionary. I take off my hat to him." He made a symbolic gesture, his long black hair falling momentarily over his face.
>
> Another long silence.
>
> Then suddenly Borodin whirled, his face contorted with fury as he shook his fist in my face. "But where do you find him today?" he shouted. "Answer me that. Where do you find him? Where? Where? Where?"
>
> Then furiously, but triumphantly: "You can't answer me!" (*Chou,* pp. 34-35)

Where are they? They certainly are not among those who think Christianity exists solely for their health, wealth, and happiness. Neither are they among those who conform to the world, making their place in the lukewarm spiritual mediocrity—indistinguishable from the world system.

Where are they? They are those who have made such a radical identification with Christ that they are His very eyes and hands and lips. They are the ones who risk a word for Him when it may mean rejection. They are the people who speak up for righteousness though it may cost them dearly. They are the men and women who submit their own comfort to the ministry of Christ's love in a dying world.

11
The Convicting Work
of the Holy Spirit
John 16:5-16

Because of the self-centeredness of our time, there is a danger-ous tendency among Christians to imagine that those who are faithfully following Christ will always experience good health, wealth, and ease. This is not true. Because Christ's followers are not of the world system, they can expect to experience the enmity of that system.

William Tyndale, who gave us the English Bible, once said about the persecution he had suffered, "I never expected any-thing else" (William Barclay, *The Gospel of John,* Westminster Press, vol. 2, p. 221). The more authentic our Christian walk, the more likely we are to be persecuted. The Apostle Paul wrote to Timothy: "And indeed, all who desire to live godly in Christ Jesus will be persecuted" (2 Tim. 3:12).

As Jesus continued with His disciples in the Upper Room, He began to talk with them about the fact that He was going to leave them. It was hard for their troubled hearts to believe that His leaving would be good for them, as He said:

"But now I am going to Him who sent Me; and none of you asks Me, 'Where are You going?' But because I have said these things to you, sorrow has filled your heart. But I tell you the truth, it is to your advantage that I go away; for if I do not go away, the

Helper shall not come to you; but if I go, I will send Him to you"
(John 16:5-7).

How incredible His words must have sounded to the disciples. Judas had already slipped out into the night. Some of Jesus' words had been dark with portent. He had already predicted Peter's denial. The world system was plotting death to their Master. Sorrow had filled their hearts. And then Jesus said that His leaving would be a good thing.

The disciples were to come to understand what He meant, that the Holy Spirit would be alongside of them, encouraging them, teaching them, carrying the presence of Christ to each of them.

However, the Holy Spirit would do more than that. He would be sent to convict the world and to comfort the believers.

"But I tell you the truth, it is to your advantage that I go away; for if I do not go away, the Helper shall not come to you; but if I go, I will send Him to you. And He, when He comes, will convict the world concerning sin, and righteousness, and judgment" (16:7-8).

Apart from the Holy Spirit, mankind does not understand spiritual realities. His ministry is to bring to the world a correct perception of three realities—of sin, of righteousness, and of judgment.

Many people believe that what they don't know won't hurt them. But that is far from true. Even on the most mundane level, what we don't know can work great harm in our lives. This is illustrated by a story that is said to have happened in southern Texas about the turn of the century.

Jorge Rodriguez was a Mexican bank robber who operated along the Texas border. He was so successful in his raids that the Texas Rangers assigned an extra posse to the Rio Grande to stop him. Late one afternoon, one of the special rangers saw Jorge slipping stealthily across the river and followed him as he returned to his home village. The ranger watched as Jorge first mingled with the townspeople in the square around the well, and then went into his favorite cantina to relax. The ranger slipped into the cantina and managed to get the drop on Jorge. With a pistol to Jorge's head, he said, "I know who you are, Jorge Rodriguez, and I have come to get back all the money you have stolen from the banks in Texas. Give it to me, or I am going to pull the trigger."

There was just one problem—Jorge didn't speak English and the ranger didn't speak Spanish. At that moment, a villager came over and said, "I am bilingual. Shall I act as translator?" The ranger nodded, and the villager proceeded to put the words of the ranger into terms that Jorge could understand.

Nervously, Jorge answered, "Tell the big Texas ranger that I have not spent a cent of the money. If he will go to the town well, face north, count down five stones, he will find a loose stone. If he pulls it out, he will find all the money. Please tell him quickly."

The translator assumed a solemn look and turned to the ranger. "Jorge Rodriguez is a brave man. He says he is ready to die" (John R. Claypool, *The Preaching Event,* Word Books, pp. 121-122).

What Jorge didn't know did hurt him! He needed a faithful translator. This is what Jesus was promising to His disciples, a faithful translator of His truth in the Person of the Holy Spirit. Our ignorance of sin, righteousness, and judgment will ultimately bring eternal hurt. The Holy Spirit comes to convict, to cross-examine, with the purpose of convincing or refuting an opponent. "He does not simply convict the world . . . but will show that it is lacking in knowledge of what sin and righteousness really are" (B.F. Westcott, *The Gospel According to St. John,* Wm. B. Eerdmans, p. 229).

Conviction of Sin

The Holy Spirit convicts the world "concerning sin because they do not believe in Me" (16:9). The Spirit brings the guilt of sin home to the human consciousness so that men and women will seek relief. We see an example of this on the Day of

Pentecost. The believers had been gathered together for many days, but not until the Holy Spirit came did they go out to preach. At the end of Peter's first sermon, he said:

> "Therefore let all the house of Israel know for certain that God has made Him both Lord and Christ—this Jesus whom you crucified." Now when they heard this, they were pierced to the heart, and said to Peter and the rest of the apostles, "Brethren, what shall we do?" (Acts 2:36-37)

The response was amazing. But Peter's eloquence or sermon structure or cleverness of argument had nothing to do with it. The convicting power of the Holy Spirit elicited the reaction. The listeners' hearts were pierced unto salvation.

In his book, *The Holy Spirit,* Dr. R. A. Torrey tells of when he was pastor of Moody Church in Chicago. The church had a twenty-five member committee of elders and deacons. The committee met every Friday evening for supper and to go over the church rolls to see which people needed attention. At one meeting, an elder expressed a concern:

> Brethren, I am not at all satisfied with the way things are going in our church. We are having many professed conversions, and we are having many accessions to the Church, but I do not see the conviction of sin that I would like to see. I propose that, instead of discussing business matters any further tonight, we spend the time in prayer, and that we meet on other nights also, to cry to God to send His Holy Spirit among us in convicting power (Fleming H. Revell, p. 45).

Everyone consented and they spent not only the rest of that evening in prayer, but a number of the following nights, asking for the Spirit's convicting power. Not long after that first meeting, as Dr. Torrey rose one Sunday evening to preach, he saw seated to his left a professional gambler. As he preached, he saw that the man's eyes were riveted on him with unusual attention. After the meeting, one of the church leaders brought the gambler to Dr. Torrey. The man's opening words were, "Oh, I don't know what's the matter with me. I feel awful." He told how that afternoon he was out walking and saw an open-air meeting. Among the participants was a man he had formerly known in his gambling pursuits. He stopped to listen but wasn't much impressed and went his way. Yet, after he had walked several blocks, some mysterious power moved him to return. After the open-air meeting, he was invited to church, and so had heard Dr. Torrey. Now he was invited to go downstairs in Moody Church to talk further.

The gambler groaned again, "Oh, I don't know what's the matter with me. I never felt like this before. I feel awful," and he trembled like a leaf.

Dr. Torrey said, "I'll tell you what's the matter with you. The Holy Spirit is convicting you of sin."

Trembling with deep emotion, that gambler knelt and cried to God for mercy. He left the church with the joyous realization that his sins were all forgiven (Torrey, *The Holy Spirit,* Revell, p. 47).

The convicting power of the Holy Spirit ... the phrase describes what was working on me as a twelve-year-old boy. I had sat under the preaching of the Word for several months and became increasingly aware of my own sinfulness, until I imagined that I was too sinful for Christ to take me. I actually thought that He could save others, but not me. Then one night after a meeting, I shyly approached the preacher to talk with him about my soul, and it was then that I found Jesus. All because of the marvelous convicting power of the Holy Spirit.

The convicting work of the Holy Spirit focuses primarily on the sin of unbelief. The average unbeliever does not look on his unbelief as sin. However, when he is brought under the Spirit's conviction, he has to focus on this. It was Pascal who said, "Man is great insofar as he is wretched." For only as we see the wretchedness of our sin can we come into the blessedness of God's grace.

Conviction of Righteousness

The second convicting work of the Holy Spirit is to show us the righteousness provided in Christ. Jesus said the Spirit would do this, because He was going to the Father and they would no longer behold Him (16:10). The world has a relative view of righteousness, generally perceiving God's righteousness and man's righteousness as merely different levels of the same thing. Righteousness is regarded in percentages, with God holding 100 percent and good to bad men possessing relative amounts. The logical outcome of this view is the unfortunate assumption that there is a degree of righteousness which will be acceptable to God, and that if man attains it, he will attain heaven.

But Jesus demonstrated and taught an entirely new standard of righteousness. His repeated statements revealed the profoundness and depth of the inner righteousness necessary to enter the kingdom of God. He emphasized that to attain this righteousness man had to come to the end of himself. In the Sermon on the Mount He said, "Unless your righteousness surpasses that of the scribes and Pharisees, you shall not enter the kingdom of heaven" (Matt. 5:20).

How discouraging, for the Pharisees were the spiritual athletes of the day. The sum of the Sermon on the Mount was this: "Therefore, you are to be perfect, as your heavenly Father is perfect" (Matt. 5:48). The only righteousness acceptable to the kingdom is perfection.

Our Lord's teaching would be vindicated when He was accepted back into heaven by His Father—"concerning righteousness, because I go to the Father" (16:10). When God raised Jesus from the dead, He was saying, "This is the Man I accept, and all men unlike Him I reject." The Resurrection was the evidence in human history of the type, the pattern, that God accepts.

The Holy Spirit convinces us that our own righteousness doesn't come close to Jesus' righteousness. When we are so convicted, we abandon the syndrome of ever trying harder. We abandon all hope in salvation through our percentage ratings of human righteousness. We see that all the ground at the foot of the cross is level. And with the Apostle Paul, we pray that we may be found in Him, "not having a righteousness of our own derived from the law, but that which is through faith in Christ, the righteousness which comes from God on the basis of faith" (Phil. 3:9).

The person who is in the process of coming to grace is deeply aware of his personal unworthiness. Only the Holy Spirit can bring this awareness. Are you convinced of your sin? Are you convinced of Christ's righteousness? If so, you are either within God's grace or almost there. And if the Holy Spirit has convinced you of sin and of righteousness, the third conviction follows.

Conviction of Judgment

The Holy Spirit convinces the world that there is such a thing as judgment. The judgment of Satan on the Cross, and the breaking of his power, is proof of that. Jesus said that the Spirit would convict "concerning judgment, because the ruler of this world has been judged" (16:11).

When Jesus was on the Cross, Satan threw at Him every power at his disposal, but Jesus rose from the dead. "When He ascended on high, He led captive a host of captives, and He gave gifts to men" (Eph. 4:8). Christ led a victory parade. Satan only bruised Christ's heel, but Christ crushed Satan's head. Therefore, Christ will now bring judgment on those who are part of the world system. He is the ineluctable Judge.

When I was twelve years old and under conviction, I knew very little about sin. I hadn't committed any awful sins, but I did know that I was a sinner, that Jesus' righteousness was something I could never match, and that I was under judgment. Someone might say, "What a terrible load for a young boy to carry!" Actually, it was the birth of my liberation. "The hardness of God is kinder than the softness of men, and His compulsion is our liberation" (C. S. Lewis, *Surprised by Joy*. Harcourt, Brace & World, p. 229).

Are you experiencing the hardness of God? Are you truly under conviction of sin? Do you have a compulsion to find relief?

You may be coming to liberation. If so, thank God for this conviction.

Conviction through Believers

The work of the Holy Spirit is to convict the world of sin, righteousness, and judgment. It is His work, not ours. There is nothing you and I can do to bring conviction. But while it is the Spirit's work, He accomplishes this work through us.

> "But I tell you the truth, it is to your advantage that I go away, for if I do not go away, the Helper shall not come to you; but if I go, I will send him to you. And He, when He comes [to you], will convict the world concerning sin and righteousness and judgment" (16:7-8).

As far as we know, the British philosopher Thomas Huxley never put his faith in Christ, but he did experience some degree of conviction. Toward the end of the last century, he was a guest at a house party in the country. Sunday came and most of the guests prepared to go to church, but Huxley did not propose to go. Instead, he approached a man known to have a simple and radiant Christian faith and said to him, "Suppose you don't go to church today. Suppose you stay at home and tell me quite simply what your Christian faith means to you and why you are a Christian."

The man replied, "But you could demolish my arguments in an instant. I am not clever enough to argue with you."

Huxley said gently, "I don't want to argue with you; I just want you to tell me simply what this Christ means to you."

The man stayed home and told Huxley of his faith. When he had finished, there were tears in the great agnostic's eyes. "I would give my right hand," he said, "if only I could believe that" (William Barclay, *The Gospel of John*. Westminster Press, vol. 1, p. 76).

Maybe this idea that God uses people to bring men under conviction was behind Paul's words to the Corinthians:

You are our letter, written in our hearts, known and read by all men; being manifested that you are a letter of Christ, cared for by us, written not with ink, but with the Spirit of the living God, not on tablets of stone, but on tablets of human hearts (2 Cor. 3:2-3).

While I was dating my wife, we lived far enough apart that we corresponded some. When I received one of her letters, I would drop everything and read it, reread it, and then read it again. Sometimes I would even let my roommate read part of a letter, but once was always enough for him. It was different for me, for I knew her life, and there was as much for me between the lines as in what she had written. This is the way it is with our lives. They are open letters to be known and read by all men. And when they are authentic in identification with Christ, they convict men of the sin that is theirs, of the righteousness that may be theirs, and of the judgment that they will face.

Comfort for Believers

"But when He, the Spirit of truth, comes, He will guide you into all the truth; for He will not speak on His own initiative, but whatever He hears, He will speak; and He will disclose to you what is to come. He shall glorify Me; for He shall take of Mine, and shall disclose it to you. All things that the Father has are Mine; therefore I said, that He takes of Mine, and will disclose it to you" (16:13-15).

The Holy Spirit will guide us into "all the truth." We will grow as He further illuminates the Scriptures. This doesn't mean that we will have all knowledge regarding the sciences, but that we will be taken deeper and deeper into the essential truth. The expression, "all the truth," connotes increasing liberation as the truth makes us free. We increasingly have the mind of Christ, as the Spirit takes what is Christ's and discloses it to us.

But just as it is written, "Things which eye has not seen and ear has not heard, and which have not entered the heart of man, all that God has prepared for those who love Him." For to us God revealed them through the Spirit; for the Spirit searches all things, even the depths of God (1 Cor. 2:9-10).

The Holy Spirit's work is to open our eyes and enlarge our ability to see. He must always begin with sin and righteousness and judgment.

Many years ago, a young woman sat in church. Like so many people today, she understood the great doctrines, but considered herself unworthy.

She was almost in despair and hardly heard the words of the elderly man who was speaking. Suddenly, right in the middle of his address, the preacher stopped and, pointing his finger at her, said, "You, Miss, sitting there at the back, you can be saved *now.* You don't need to do anything!" His words struck like thunder in her heart. She believed at once, and with her belief there came a wonderful sense of peace and real joy. That night Charlotte Elliott went home and wrote the well-known hymn:

> Just as I am, without one plea
> But that Thy blood was shed for me,
> And that Thou bidd'st me come to Thee,
>   O Lamb of God, I come.
>   (James M. Boice, *The Gospel of John,*
>   Zondervan, vol. 1, pp. 392-93)

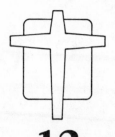

12
From Sorrow to Joy

John 16:16-33

For the true believer, the sorrows of life are pregnant with potential for joy. Those who live with faith in the resurrection have gone through the transformation from sorrow to joy. As they came to know Christ, their mourning over sins was turned to joy. And it is the continuing experience of Christian growth that difficulties do spawn joy.

It is hard to imagine the misery the disciples must have felt that last night in the Upper Room with Jesus, as they saw their Master in the hours before His death, apparently helpless against the coming doom.

What is significant for us, as well as for them, is that Jesus didn't replace their sorrow with something more desirable. He transformed the sorrow into joy.

Joy and Sorrow

"Truly, truly, I say to you, that you will weep and lament, but the world will rejoice; you will be sorrowful, but your sorrow will be turned to joy" (John 16:20).

Jesus Himself experienced this same transformation in His life, as His deepest sorrow became the source of His greatest joy. Isaiah 53:3 says, "He was despised and forsaken of men, a man of sorrows, and acquainted with grief." But Hebrews 12:2 describes Him as One "who for the joy set before Him endured the cross." The miracle of the Cross transformed sorrow into joy for Jesus' disciples. It can work the same miracle in us.

Dr. R. A. Torrey gives a memorable testimony concerning the mysterious working of this transformation in his life. When their twelve-year-old daughter died of diphtheria, Dr. Torrey and his wife went through a time of great heartache. The funeral was held on a miserable, rainy day. As they stood near her little grave and watched her body being buried, Mrs. Torrey said, "I'm so glad Elizabeth is with the Lord and not in that box." Yet despite this knowledge, their hearts were broken. As Dr. Torrey told it, the next day as he was walking down the street, the misery came to him anew. He felt the loneliness that lay ahead, the heartbreak of an empty house. In his misery he cried aloud, "Oh, Elizabeth! Elizabeth!"

> And just then this fountain, the Holy Spirit, that I had in my heart, broke forth with such power as I think I had never experienced before, and it was the most joyful moment I had ever known in my life. Oh, how wonderful is the joy of the Holy Ghost! It is an unspeakably glorious thing to have your joy not in things about you, not even in your most dearly loved friends, but to have within you a fountain ever springing up, springing up, springing up, always springing up, springing up under all circumstances into everlasting life (*The Holy Spirit*, R. A. Torrey, Fleming H. Revell, p. 95).

In that moment, Dr. Torrey experienced a supernatural touch that transformed sorrow to joy. It was not that he no longer mourned, no longer missed his daughter—for I am sure that her death brought some pain for as long as he lived—but that he had entered into the transforming power that the Cross and Resurrection bring to the Christian.

To illustrate what the transformation would be like, Jesus used the phenomenon of giving birth:

"Whenever a woman is in travail she has sorrow, because her hour has come; but when she gives birth to the child, she remembers the anguish no more, for joy that a child has been born into the world" (16:21).

He didn't mean that a woman who has given birth can't remember the pain of childbirth. Rather that the joy of a new child thrusts the pain into the background.

We see this principle at work in the lives of great biblical heroes. Moses' forty years of discouragement were followed by fort˙ years of powerful ministry. Abraham's despair over the barrenness of Sarah ultimately ended in joyous song.

As people of like faith and heritage, and as children of the same God, our present difficulties bear potential for joy. True, some of us will never know the complete joy until we are with the Lord; but even in life, our sorrows bear the potential of a transformed and deeper joy. In the consummate difficulties of life there can be a transforming power that brings joy, a new and different kind of joy, even for broken families, even in spite of financial reversals.

Jesus told His disciples that this joy would be a present possession. "Therefore you, too, now have sorrow; but I will see you again, and your heart will rejoice, and no one takes your joy away from you" (16:22). The disciples experienced exactly what Jesus predicted. And so did believers in generations to follow.

This is why Paul could write from prison, "Rejoice in the Lord always; again I will say, rejoice!" (Phil. 4:4) He reiterated variations of this theme ten times in his Epistle to the Philippians. Nothing could take away his joy. This is the experience of faithful believers. They have joy and comfort that the angels cannot give and devils cannot take.

Jesus knew that the lives of His disciples would be filled with continuing difficulty. He warned them of this in both the opening and closing verses of John 16. Along with the promise of sorrow being turned to joy, Christ also spoke about the maintenance of that transforming joy and peace through proper actions and mind-set.

Joy and Prayer

> "And in that day you will ask Me no question. Truly, truly, I say
> to you, if you shall ask the Father for anything, He will give it
> to you in My name. Until now you have asked for nothing in My
> name; ask, and you will receive, that your joy may be made full"
> (16:23-24).

Before the Cross, the disciples either asked Jesus directly or
prayed to the Father, as Christ taught them to pray. After the
Cross, a new arrangement was inaugurated. The disciples were
to ask in Jesus' name. And that is why we pray in Jesus' name.

This concept has often been misunderstood. Some people
have interpreted it to mean that by tagging Jesus' name on the
end of their prayers, they could ask for anything they wished
and they would get it. It has often been used as an excuse to
pursue material gain: "Lord, I want a Rolls Silver Cloud and a
villa on Majorca, and I'm asking God for these. It says right here
that if I ask in Jesus' name. . . ."

It is true that we are to pray in Jesus' name and this has
everything to do with our joy continuing and being made full.
But asking in His name brings some constraints. First, it means
that we do not come in our own names. Dr. James Boice has
said:

> Much modern prayer, even by serious Christian people, is use-
> less and ineffective because the people involved approach God
> thinking that He is obliged to grant their requests because of
> something they have themselves done for Him (*The Gospel of
> John*, vol. IV, Zondervan, p. 314).

Praying in Christ's name means coming only in His merit, not
our own. Christ's full name is Lord Jesus Christ, which means
Jehovah, Saviour, God's Anointed. It is this name whose merit
we most humbly pray. We cannot think that somehow God will
hear us because of our virtue. We come by virtue of His merit.
Poverty of spirit is the basis on which we approach God, and our
ongoing poverty is the ground of blessing. If we learn this, if

we come to God in poverty of spirit, we can expect our prayers to be answered.

The second requirement of praying in Jesus' name is that we pray in correspondence with Christ's character and objectives. Oswald Chambers interprets praying in Christ's name as asking anything that is according to Christ's nature. This means that we are to pray for what Christ would want, not necessarily our spontaneous desires. Prayer is not a means by which we get God to do what we want. Rather, it is a means by which God does through us what He wants. Chambers says, "The idea of prayer is not in order to get answers from God; prayer is perfect and complete oneness with God" (*My Utmost for His Highest,* Dodd, Mead & Co., p. 150).

This kind of praying happens when we are filled with the Holy Spirit and our hearts are so in tune with the Lord that we pray for those things He desires for us. Paul tells us:

> The Spirit also helps our weakness; for we do not know how to pray as we should, but the Spirit Himself intercedes for us with groanings too deep for words; and He who searches the hearts knows what the mind of the Spirit is, because He intercedes for the saints according to the will of God (Rom. 8:26-27).

When we truly pray in His name, there is a sense in which we actually articulate the Spirit's hidden intercession. As we pray in His nature, we find answers to our prayers and we experience increased joy.

The final requirement for praying in Jesus' name is submission to Him. This means that we yield to the process of the Cross and the Resurrection, death and life, sorrow and joy. We must submit to this process or we are not really submitting to Jesus' name. Alan Redpath says, "When God wants to use a man, He takes him and crushes him." Submission to Jesus allows our sorrows to be turned to joy.

When our prayers are answered as we ask, we know a special joy. Jesus spoke of this, "Until now you have asked for nothing in My name; ask, and you will receive, that your joy may be made full" (16:24).

Think of the changes in a life when there is repeated asking in His name with the resultant refilling of joy. This is what the disciples were told to look for. It has been the way of life of countless believers.

Prayer in Jesus' name is to lead us to direct relationship with the Father, so that we will also know His love for us:

> "In that day you will ask in My name; and I do not say to you that I will request the Father on your behalf; for the Father Himself loves you, because you have loved Me, and have believed that I came forth from the Father" (16:26-27).

Joy and Belief

There is also a relationship between joy and belief. Notice Jesus' teaching about His mission, and the disciples' response:

> "I came forth from the Father, and have come into the world; I am leaving the world again, and going to the Father."
>
> His disciples said, "Lo, now You are speaking plainly and are not using a figure of speech. Now we know that You know all things, and have no need for anyone to question You; by this we believe that You came from God" (16:28-30).

The disciples were pleased with themselves, for they understood something of the ministry of the Holy Spirit. They had heard that He would transform sorrow to joy. They had listened to Jesus' teaching about prayer and they had been assured of God's love. But their knowledge was still shallow.

So the Lord asked the big question: "Do you now believe?" (16:31) It is a question we all must face. Do we really believe what He has said? Do we really believe what we say we believe? About His joy-transforming process of life? About His call to joy-giving prayer?

Christ concluded with this statement, His final words in the Upper Room before His farewell prayer:

> "Behold, an hour is coming, and has already come, for you to be scattered, each to his own home, and to leave Me alone; and

yet I am not alone, because the Father is with Me. These things I have spoken to you, that in Me you may have peace. In the world you have tribulation, but take courage; I have overcome the world" (16:32-33).

These were courageous, audacious words, spoken in the face of the demonic hordes He would encounter in the following hours. How could Christ say them? Because He believed His sorrow would be turned to joy! Because He believed the disciples' sorrow would be also. Because He believed that as they prayed in His name, their joy would multiply. Because He believed the Father loved them.

And He says to us today, "Do you now believe? Then cheer up! It is a fact that I have overcome the world!"

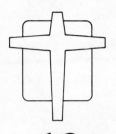

13
The Holy of Holies
John 17:1-19

John 17 is one of the most treasured chapters in the Bible. It has been called the holy of holies of Sacred Scripture, for in it Christ bares His heart in final public prayer to His Father before He steps out into the night to proceed to the cross.

Philip Melancthon, one of the towering intellects of the early Reformation, said:

> There is no voice which has ever been heard, either in heaven or in earth, more exalted, more holy, more fruitful, more sublime, than the prayer offered up by the Son of God Himself (quoted by A. W. Pink, *Exposition of the Gospel of John,* Vol. III, Zondervan, p. 90).

This chapter was read to the Scottish reformer, John Knox, every day during his final illness and even in his final moments. The chapter has been the inspiration of massive works and numberless sermons. As we enter, may we do so with the sense that we are on holy ground.

The arrangement of the prayer is easy to follow, as it breaks into three divisions. In verses 1-5 Christ prays for Himself and His own glorification. In verses 6-19 He remembers His apostles, and in verses 20-25 He prays for the church in the world.

Christ Prays for Himself

As Christ prays for His own glorification, He asks that His glory be manifested in three ways—on the cross, in heaven, and in the church.

His desire for glorification through the cross is expressed in verse 1:

> "Father, the hour has come; glorify Thy Son, that the Son may glorify Thee."

Both Christ and His Father would be glorified on the cross because the cross would supremely reveal their nature and purpose. Jesus is the explanation of the Father (John 1:18). What people learn of Christ on the cross, they also learn of the Father.

The cross is the diagram of the love of both Father and Son. Our knowledge of this love would be impossible without the cross and this is why Christ prayed for the cross.

Christ also prayed for His own glorification in heaven:

> "And now, glorify Thou Me together with Thyself, Father, with the glory which I ever had with Thee before the world was" (17:5).

Before the world was, Jesus existed in ineffable glory. He was the Creator of a universe so large that it would take fifty octillion years traveling at the speed of light to visit every star. In the glory of His being, He enjoyed perfect intimacy with the Godhead in the continuous, joyous oneness of the Father, Son, and Holy Spirit. Beyond this, we know little—except that He decided to empty Himself of this glory, to make the incredible plunge of the Incarnation.

Jesus' return to the unspeakable magnificence of His original glory would be enhanced by further honor which He acquired here on earth. Our Lord has an even greater glory as He reigns in His glorified human body at the right hand of the Father, beautified by those scars He received to redeem us. His glory is not greater in scope, perhaps, since infinite cannot be enlarged. But it is greater in that it is better understood by men and angels.

Christ then prays for glorification through future believers who would know Him.

> "That to all whom Thou hast given Him, He may give eternal life. And this is eternal life, that they may know Thee, the only true God, and Jesus Christ whom Thou hast sent" (17:2-3).

This *knowing* Christ speaks of is an intimate relationship with Him. The Old Testament regularly uses the word *know* for sexual knowledge, as in "Adam knew Eve his wife; and she conceived, and bare Cain" (Gen. 4:1, KJV). The idea of knowing, therefore, suggests a mutual experience and exchange. Knowing Christ is not simply knowing something about Him, but means having a personal knowledge of Him. Truly converted people *know* Jesus and Jesus knows them. Christ is alive in their lives, and this intimate life glorifies God.

Jesus asked for three things: glorification through the cross, reglorification in heaven, and glory through His people who know Him intimately. For those who are His, this is a compelling call to know Him even more intimately.

True believers all show Christ to some degree and in some way. But there are those who, by their deep knowledge of Him, seem at times to *be* Christ. What a glory they are to Him!

Christ Prays for His Disciples

In verses 6-19 the prayer moves to petition for Christ's devoted disciples. In verses 6-10, Christ seems to be introducing or presenting His disciples to His Father, as He prays on their behalf.

> "I manifested Thy name to the men whom Thou gavest Me out of the world; Thine they were, and Thou gavest them to Me, and they have kept Thy word. Now they have come to know that everything Thou hast given Me is from Thee; for the words

which Thou gavest Me I have given to them; and they received them, and truly understood that I came forth from Thee, and they believed that Thou didst send Me. I ask on their behalf; I do not ask on behalf of the world, but of those whom Thou hast given Me; for they are Thine; and all things that are Mine are Thine, and Thine are Mine; and I have been glorified in them" (17:6-10).

In verses 11-19, we see specific requests Christ makes for His disciples—about how they relate to one another and how they relate to the nonbelieving world.

• Relating to other Christians. Our Lord knew His followers were going to have trouble. There had been the repeated childish squabbles, as when James and John and their mother tried to obtain the best thrones in the kingdom. Or when Peter asked how much forgiveness he should extend to a brother, suggesting that seven times was a generous offer. Jesus had replied, "I do not say to you, up to seven times, but up to seventy times seven" (Matt. 18:22). That was beyond the disciples' comprehension, and to such teaching their reply was, "Increase our faith!" (Luke 17:5)

Now, as Christ looked into the centuries ahead, He saw Christians breaking fellowship with their brothers over matters like the mode of baptism—three times forward or one time backward? Or the color of the church bathrooms. Every age has known division. The Puritan Thomas Brookes wrote: "For wolves to worry the lambs is no wonder, but for one lamb to worry another, this is unnatural and monstrous" (I. D. E. Thomas, *Puritan Quotations,* Moody Press, p. 304).

Jesus prayed that oneness would be maintained by the disciples being kept in the Father's name:

"And I am no more in the world; and yet they themselves are in the world, and I come to Thee. Holy Father, keep them in Thy name, the name which Thou hast given Me, that they may be one, even as We are. While I was with them, I was keeping them in Thy name which Thou hast given Me; and I guarded them, and not one of them perished but the son of perdition, that the Scripture might be fulfilled" (17:11-12).

The security and unity of Christ's followers comes from being kept in the Father's name. Names were significant to the Jewish people. To them, a name was representative of a person's character. This is why the psalmist commented, "Some boast in chariots, and some in horses; but we will boast in the name of the Lord our God" (Ps. 20:7). Jesus built oneness and a sense of security among the disciples by showing both in His life and His teaching the personality and character of the Father. The more the disciples understood the attributes and character of God, the more they experienced unity. A. W. Tozer illustrated it this way:

> Has it ever occurred to you that one hundred pianos all tuned to the same fork are automatically tuned to each other? They are of one accord by being tuned, not to each other, but to another standard to which each one must individually bow. So one hundred worshippers met together, each one looking away to Christ, are in heart nearer to each other than they could possibly be were they to become "unity" conscious and turn their eyes away from God to strive for closer fellowship (*The Pursuit of God*, Tyndale, p. 97).

The more we know of God, the more we are drawn to Him and the more we are then drawn to one another. The emphasis of the words here suggests something very precious. While Jesus prayed that the whole character of God be kept before the disciples, the emphasis was on the fatherhood of God: "Holy Father, keep them in Thy name." Handley C. G. Moule, one-time Lord Bishop of Durham, said:

> *In Thy Name;* they were never to be allowed to wander out of that Name; never to seek another name, one of their own imagining or developing; never to dream of safety or of home for their souls anywhere but within the revealed personal love and life of the holy Father of our Lord Jesus Christ. Within the mystical circle of a knowledge of God as Father they were to be "preserved" (*The High Priestly Prayer*, Baker Book House, pp. 101-102).

The contemplation and appropriation of the blessed truth that God is our Father thrusts us toward oneness. Those who have the same father long for and love their brothers and sisters. Oneness is a growing reality, and the result of oneness is joy.

"But now I come to Thee; and these things I speak in the world, that they may have My joy made full in themselves" (17:13).

Jesus was praying for the joy which has its origin in heaven. Joy is the serious business of heaven, its occupation and realization. Joy like this is not dependent on circumstances.

As Jesus prayed for our relationships with each other, He asked that we will be constantly growing in the knowledge of God. For then we will be growing in oneness, and this will result in joy.

• Relating to the world. How are Christ's followers to relate to the world? Especially if they are living in unity with one another?

"I have given them Thy word; and the world has hated them, because they are not of the world, even as I am not of the world" (17:14).

Christians will have trouble in the world, just as Jesus did. In fact the more they are like Jesus, the more trouble they will have. What is Jesus' answer to this: "I do not ask Thee to take them out of the world, but to keep them from the evil one" (17:15). This suggests three attitudes.

—Not isolation. The Christian attitude toward the world should not be one of withdrawal. Christ does not ask that we be taken away. Withdrawal has always been a religious temptation. In Jesus' time the Pharisees succumbed to this temptation. The term *Pharisee* means separatist. The goal of the Pharisees was to escape the contamination of a fallen society. In the third century, Christian hermits fled to the deserts of Egypt. This mentality was perpetuated in the rise of monasticism in the

Middle Ages, and vestiges of this mind-set can still be seen today in orders such as the Carthusians or the hermits of the Eastern Church.

We have all had inclinations to withdraw. When life gets rough, we say with the psalmist, "O that I had wings like a dove! I would fly away and be at rest" (Ps. 55:6). We all have escape fantasies. . . .a hideaway cabin in the north woods, burning our neckties and ordering all our clothes from the Bean catalog. I saw a bumper sticker that said, "Have you hugged your hang glider today?"

Withdrawal is a serious problem today because our Christian lifestyle can become monastic and escapist. We can arrange our lives so that we are with nonbelievers as little as possible. We can attend religious functions that we think are 100 percent Christian. We can develop a crypto-Christian language with Christian jokes, biblical nicknames, and passwords. It can happen in the most unlikely environments—even on a secular campus. Rebecca Manley Pippert, a national consultant in evangelism with Inter-Varsity Christian Fellowship, writes:

> We must not become, as John Stott puts it, "a rabbit-hole Christian"—the kind who pops his head out of a hole, leaves his Christian roommate in the morning and scurries to class, only to frantically search for a Christian to sit by (an odd way to approach a mission field). Thus he proceeds from class to class. When dinner comes, he sits with the Christians in his dorm at one huge table and thinks, "What a witness!" From there he goes to his all-Christian Bible study, and he might even catch a prayer meeting where the Christians pray for the nonbelievers on his floor. (But what luck that he was able to live on the only floor with seventeen Christians!) Then at night he scurries back to his Christian roommate. Safe! He made it through the day and his only contacts with the world were those mad, brave dashes to and from Christian activities.
>
> What an insidious reversal of the biblical command to be salt and light to the world (*Out of the Salt Shaker,* InterVarsity, Rebecca Manley Pippert, p. 124).

It is possible to go from womb to tomb in a hermetically sealed container decorated with fish stickers. It is possible to abandon our culture to the devil.

Are you aware that Moses, Elijah, and Jonah all asked to be taken out of the world? God did not grant their requests (Num. 11:15; 1 Kings 19:4; Jonah 4:3, 8). We need to examine our lives to see if we have functionally removed ourselves from the world. Christ prayed that we wouldn't do this.

—Not assimilation. The Christian attitude should not be one of conformity that molds us to the world. Christ prayed that the Father would keep us from the evil one. "They are not of the world, even as I am not of the world" (17:16). Today the temptation to conform is as great as it has ever been, particularly when Christianity is criticized for being insular. Yet sometimes conformity has been inspired by high motivation—like the desire to demonstrate the fullness of humanity which Christ brings, or a desire to be attractive to the unregenerate world, or even to suffer with the world. But the result of conformity is assimilation so that, in time, there is no distinguishable difference between us and the world. This is particularly true in a philosophical sense of those who have attempted to practice a "secular Christianity." The outcome of their effort is "Lot's tragedy," the despair of the father who earnestly warned his children of the destruction to come, only to have them think he was joking (Gen. 19:14).

On the matter of conformity, the divine charge given by the Apostle Paul still stands:

> I urge you therefore, brethren, by the mercies of God, to present your bodies a living and holy sacrifice, acceptable to God, which is your spiritual service of worship. And do not be conformed to this world, but be transformed by the renewing of your mind, that you may prove what the will of God is, that which is good and acceptable and perfect (Rom. 12:1-2).

—But mission. We can follow a steady course, without veering off to either isolation from the world or assimilation with the world. The Christian attitude toward the world is to be one of mission. Notice Christ's words: "As Thou didst send Me into the world, I also have sent them into the world" (17:18).

I had an unplanned encounter with a kind of mission a few years ago. It was while we were still living in California. One afternoon I called home from my office and my wife told me that someone from the Youth Soccer Association had called, wondering if I would be a coach that season. I said to Barbara, "Well, you told them no, didn't you?"

She replied, "I just didn't have the heart to say no. You'll have to tell them yourself." I assured her that I would be very firm. By the time I got home I had all my reasons laid out—I didn't have time, I didn't know one thing about soccer, and I really didn't want to.

I returned the call with my reasons ready, but after I had talked to the woman at the other end of the line, I realized that there wouldn't be a team if I didn't coach. I still remember my family chuckling in the background as they heard me say, "Yes, I'll do it." And there was one good reason for coaching—I would have one of my sons on the team. But I still didn't know a thing about soccer.

The next week I was in a smoke-filled room at a draft and the players were literally chosen for me. Then I was up late many nights reading soccer books, trying to understand what a center halfback was, the off-side rule, etc. And all too soon I had a coach's whistle and was occupied three days a week after school and on Saturday afternoons.

The season didn't go very well at the beginning. With me as coach, why should it have? But fortunately, I had gotten some very good players, and the team did come together. In fact, in one of the last games, we beat the number one team in the last second of the game. Then we were in the play-offs.

On the night before the play-offs, I invited the team to my church for a potluck dinner with their parents. They all came, even both sides of some divorced parents. We had a good time together with games and skits. And I said to the group, "If it is all right with you, I would like to share something from the

Word of God." The parents agreed that it was, and I told the boys the story of David and Goliath and then applied it to them.

The next day we went into the play-offs and lost in the final minutes 1-0. But that is not the end of the story. For Sunday morning, as I stepped into the pulpit, I looked out at the congregation and saw my whole soccer team in their orange jerseys. And their parents were in church too—a Muslim family, some Jews, some Mormons, and others of varying backgrounds. That began a ministry in several of the families.

True, I didn't want to coach. I didn't have time, and I didn't know anything about soccer. But because I couldn't say no, I ended up coaching and it turned into one of the great experiences of my life. Almost by accident, I learned something new about the attitude of mission we are to have in the world. For I experienced in a down-to-earth way that we are not to live in isolated fashion or to be assimilated. Rather, we are to reach out to our world in mission. Christ gives the manner of this mission in His prayer:

"Sanctify them in the truth; Thy word is truth . . . And for their sakes I sanctify Myself, that they themselves also may be sanctified in truth" (17:17, 19).

The method of mission is sanctification and that carries two ideas. The obvious one is "to make holy." The other is "to set apart for service." Sanctification comes through the Word. We are to be made holy and set apart for service by a close examination and application of the Word of God. The Word dwelling within us guards us from isolation or assimilation and gears us for mission.

Jesus volitionally set Himself apart for service and this meant taking on human flesh. In so doing, He didn't cut Himself off from the world, nor was He assimilated. Rather, He accepted the pain and peril of entering our experience, of being vulnerable and ultimately, of suffering for us. For Jesus, mission was dangerous. In Hebrews 7:26 we read that Jesus was "separated from sinners" and in Matthew 11:19 that He was a friend of sinners. Christ prayed that His followers would have an attitude of mission, as He did. And for some of us, that means taking purposeful and decisive action to reschedule our lives so that we can meet those who need Christ.

It may mean taking a class in the park district, being active in the PTA, playing racquetball with some non-Christians, being a room mother, taking an interest in the clerks in the businesses you patronize, coaching a team, joining a community club or service club, befriending your barber or hairdresser. It may mean reaching out to some fellow students or neighbors or fellow workers.

Christ prayed, "As Thou didst send Me into the world, I also have sent them into the world" (17:18). As we move out in mission, we know that Christ, our High Priest, prays for us.

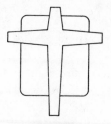

14
Christ Prays
for the Church

John 17:20-26

Christ's high priestly prayer draws concentric circles. In the inner circle (John 17:1-5), Christ prays for His glory. In the second circle (17:6-19), He prays for His disciples. In the third circle (17:20-26), He prays for His future church.

This prayer for the future church contains Christ's final words to His disciples in the Upper Room, the *terminus ad quem*. There remained yet Gethsemane and the Cross. We need this terminal perspective on His words to grasp the full impact of what Christ was saying. We also need to sense the spiraling intensity of His words. Christ did not pray this prayer dispassionately! F.B. Meyer wrote, "As the weight of the jeweled breastplate lay heavy on the heart of the high priest of old, so does it press on Him" (*The Gospel of John*, Zondervan, p. 302). The burden on Christ's soul for His future children thrust His loving heart passionately upward.

In this last section of the prayer, the flow of Christ's thoughts are: His earthly prayer for His church, His heavenly prayer for His church, and His eternal vow to His church.

That They May Be One

> "I do not ask in behalf of these alone, but for those also who believe in Me through their word; that they may all be one" (17:20-21a).

. As Jesus looked down through the centuries of His church, He prayed for its oneness. True, He was concerned about His people's love, holiness, and mission. But in His final earthly prayer, He made unity His transcending concern. Therefore, this unity must be His dominant concern today also, and we cannot overestimate its importance.

There are three important factors in Christ's earthly concern for unity: its nature, its necessity, and its means.

• Jesus was explicit about the nature of this unity. He stated it three times for emphasis:

> "That they may all be one" (17:21a).
> "That they may be one, just as We are one" (17:22b).
> "I in them, and Thou in Me, that they may be perfected in unity" (17:23a).

Christ prayed for a supernatural unity, modeled after and enabled by the Godhead. This unity was and is possible because true believers are partakers of the divine nature and are united to one another in the core of their beings. That is why we often can sense that we have met another believer before either of us has said a word. It is because we share the divine nature. Paul's words to the Colossians have helped me to understand this:

> For in Him all the fullness of Deity dwells in bodily form, and in Him you have been made complete, and He is the head over all rule and authority (Col. 2:9-10).

The closer we draw to Him, the closer we draw to one another. Our unity can be described as an inverted cone. God is at the top and believers are around the base. As we ascend the slopes of the cone, we draw closer to our fellow believers. At the pinnacle where God is, we touch one another in deepest joy. John gave this as one of his reasons for preaching the Gospel:

> What we have seen and heard we proclaim to you also, that you also may have fellowship with us; and indeed our fellowship is with the Father, and with His Son Jesus Christ. And these things we write, so that our joy may be made complete (1 John 1:3-4).

Christian unity is supernatural because it comes from God's nature and is only experienced in its fullness as we draw close to Him. Christ prayed that we would know unity in its fullness: "That they may be one, just as we are one."

However, this unity does not mean uniformity in everything. Even in the Trinity, there exists diversity in unity. There are three distinct persons, yet they are one. And that diversity is always a characteristic of the church. Let me illustrate. Suppose that by a miracle we could bring together under one roof some of the greatest Christians of the centuries. From the fourth century would come the great intellect, Augustine of Hippo. From the tenth century the saintly mystic and poet, Bernard of Clairvaux; from the sixteenth century, the peerless reformer, John Calvin. From the seventeenth century would come John Wesley, the great Methodist advocate of free will. Along with him would be the evangelist, George Whitefield. From the nineteenth century, C.H. Spurgeon and D.L. Moody. And finally, from the twentieth century, Billy Graham.

If we could gather all these men under one steeple, we would be unable to reach a unanimous opinion on very much. Yet underneath their diversity of style and theological distinctives would be unity. And the more these men lifted up Christ and focused on Him, the greater would be their unity.

Too many Christians think that other believers should be just like them—that they should all carry the same version of the Bible, read the same books, promote the same styles of ministry and life, educate their children in the same way, have the same likes and dislikes. This is uniformity, not unity. We are not called to be Christian clones. In fact, this insistence that others be just like us is one of the most disunifying forces in the church of Jesus Christ. It engenders a judgmental inflexibility which hurls people away from the church with a deadly centrifugal force.

One of the glories of the Gospel is that it hallows our individuality while bringing us into unity. This unity without uniformity is implicit in Paul's teaching on spiritual gifts.

Now there are varieties of gifts, but the same Spirit. And there are varieties of ministries, and the same Lord. And there are varieties of effects, but the same God who works all things in all persons (1 Cor. 12:4-6).

Christ prayed for unity of truth and spirit. As John Stott pointed out, the unity enjoined here is not only a unity among present believers, but a unity with the apostolic church and its teaching. Christ said that He was not asking in behalf of the apostles alone but for future believers also who would believe in Him. "I do not ask in behalf of these alone, but for those also who believe in Me through their word" (17:20).

It is first and foremost a prayer that there may be a historical continuity between the church of the first century and the church of subsequent centuries; that the church's faith may not change but remain recognizably the same; that the church of every age may merit the title "apostolic" because it is loyal to the teaching of the apostles (John Stott, *Christ the Liberator*, InterVarsity Press, pp. 82—83).

The nature of the unity for which the Saviour prayed comes from the indwelling of the Holy Spirit and grows as we scale the slopes to God, through an apostolic faith, by being rooted and strengthened in His Word. We are never closer to one another than when our hearts are genuinely focused on God.

• This pursuit of unity is necessary as we reach out to non-Christians. Our Lord explained its importance to the world in verses 21 and 23:

> "That they may all be one; even as Thou, Father, art in Me, and I in Thee, that they also may be in Us; that the world may believe that Thou didst send Me.
>
> "I in them, and Thou in Me, that they may be perfected in unity, that the world may know that Thou didst send Me, and didst love them, even as Thou didst love Me."

Unity is an evangelistic necessity, for we live in a fragmented world. When Christians have unity, the world can believe that Jesus really came from God the Father. For mankind deeply desires unity but doesn't know where to find it.

Jacques Ellul, the French sociologist, believes that the driving force behind ancient history was the desire to come together and advance in the face of disunity. Hence the rise of the city. In his book, *The Meaning of the City,* Ellul says that with the formation of cities came the practice of laying the foundation stone on the body of a human sacrifice, a practice, he maintains, we moderns have replaced with the sacrifice of millions of souls to the destructive systems of our great cities. The world's attempts to come together are at the expense of life (Wm. B. Eerdmans, 1970, pp. 28-29).

Because of the world's futile pursuit of unity, Christian unity is vitally important. When our unity is authentically demonstrated, it becomes irresistible. Real unity between Christians is a supernatural work pointing to a supernatural explanation—Jesus Christ in us.

Through Christian unity the world can come to understand that believers are loved by God even as He loved His own Son ... "that Thou didst send Me, and didst love them, even as Thou didst love Me" (17:23). The Greek meaning behind "even as" is "just as" or "to the same degree that." God loves those who are Christ's to the same degree and in the same way that

He loves Christ. How this can be possible I do not know. But what a tender comfort to our hearts! And through our unity, some in the world perceive this love. They evidently conclude from our unity and its accompanying love that believers are special objects of a supernatural love. Thomas Manton said, "Divisions in the church breed atheism in the world." As that is true, so is the converse; that unity in the church fosters belief in the world.

• Jesus implements this unity by giving us of His glory: "And the glory which Thou hast given Me I have given to them; that they may be one, just as We are one" (17:22).

> Jesus now says that He has given His followers the glory which the Father gave Him. That is to say, just as the true glory was to follow the path of lowly service culminating in the cross, so for them the true glory lay in the path of lowly service wherever it might lead them (Leon Morris, *The Gospel According to John*, Wm. B. Eerdmans, pp. 734-735).

Unity in this world is promoted by Christ's glory which is epitomized by humble service to one another. Paul's words to the Philippians capture the glorious attitude which Christ exemplified and which He wants from us:

> Do nothing from selfishness or empty conceit, but with humility of mind let each of you regard one another as more important than himself; do not merely look out for your own personal interests, but also for the interests of others. Have this attitude in yourselves which was also in Christ Jesus (Phil. 2:3-5).

Christ's earthly prayer for his church was for unity, which is first evidenced in apostolic truth. It is also a unity that is spiritual, promoted by our walk with God as we seek the heights. And it is a unity on earth between brothers and sisters, one that comes from the glory of humble service.

But the practice of this unity is something we must work at. We can see what this means in marriage. It is easy to forget that when a man and woman become one in Christ, they also need to commit themselves to oneness. For marriage should mean an ongoing commitment to communicate, to share their souls, to spend time together, to have the deepest relationship possible in body, soul, and spirit. Such a relationship is unutterably wonderful when experienced. But many people never know this, not because they do not want it, but because they are not committed to it. The same is true of our unity as Christians. We must be committed to it, committed to scaling the heights, committed to the apostolic faith, and committed to humbly serving one another.

That They May See the Glory

"Father, I desire that they also whom Thou hast given Me be with Me where I am, in order that they may behold My glory, which Thou hast given Me; for Thou didst love Me before the foundation of the world" (17:24).

Jesus prayed that one day we would be with Him in heaven and behold His glory. That is going to happen on the day when He says to us, "Welcome home!" We are going to be at the home we've always longed for, and we will find that we really have never wanted anything else. Christ's prayer asks that we will keep on beholding His glory, not simply that we will see it. And as we constantly behold His face, we are going to become like Him.

Beloved, now we are children of God, and it has not appeared as yet what we shall be. We know that, when He appears, we shall be like Him, because we shall see Him just as He is (1 John 3:2).

This is almost beyond hope and belief. Can we believe it? A better question for us now—can we have all that Christ desires for us today without believing it?

That They May Know Love

> O righteous Father, although the world has not known Thee, yet I have known Thee; and these have known that Thou didst send Me; and I have made Thy name known to them, and will make it known; that the love wherewith Thou didst love Me may be in them, and I in them" (17:25-26).

Jesus closed His prayer with a vow to the Father, which is also a promise to us. He will continue to make His name (meaning all that He is) known to us and will also increase the Father's love in us. That is His sovereign vow, which means it can be our continuing experience.

Some will know more of this in life than others. That is because they clearly see the passion of Christ's earthly prayer for His church and perceive their duty to draw near to Him, feed on His Word, and humbly serve one another. May we be part of the answer to His prayer!

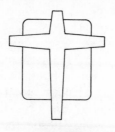

15
Who Arrested Whom?
John 18:1-11

In 1906, Albert Schweitzer published his landmark book, *The Quest for the Historical Jesus,* in which he concluded that Jesus was a mere man who was dominated by the expectation of the coming of God's kingdom, and who finally, in desperation, tried to force its coming by seeking His own death. Schweitzer describes that death in this now famous quotation:

> There is silence all around. The Baptist appears, and cries: "Repent, for the kingdom of heaven is at hand." Soon after that comes Jesus, and in the knowledge that He is the coming Son of man lays hold of the wheel of the world to set it moving on that last revolution which is to bring all ordinary history to a close. It refuses to turn, and He throws Himself upon it. Then it does turn; and crushes Him. Instead of bringing in the eschatological conditions, He has destroyed them. The wheel rolls onward, and the mangled body of the one immeasurably great Man, who was strong enough to think of Himself as the spiritual ruler of mankind and to bend history to His purpose, is hanging upon it still. That is His victory and His reign. (Macmillan, pp. 370-371).

To Schweitzer and to his followers, Jesus was a mistaken idealist, caught and crushed like a rag doll in the wheels of history. They regard Jesus' great contribution as freeing mankind of the hope of a future kingdom as it was envisioned.

Far from seeing Jesus as a helpless figure mangled on the cruel wheel of history, the Apostle John portrayed Him as One who dramatically exhibited His Lordship and control in the terrible events surrounding His death. Christ's actions have encouraging implications for us, as we also continue through a life filled with trying events.

We are going to examine Jesus' arrest and see His lordship in relation to four elements—to His surroundings, to His agony, to His antagonists, and to His purpose. In His lordship we find encouragement, for we all live in a world that appears at times to have no sovereign.

His Surroundings

The Lord chose Gethsemane as the place of encounter with His captors. John's specific mention of it as a garden—the other writers always refer to it as Gethsemane—suggests that he has in mind a comparison with the original garden, Eden. The gardens of the Bible are significant, and especially important in this comparison between Eden and Gethsemane.

> The first Adam began life in a garden;
> Christ, the second Adam, came at the end of His
>   life to a garden.
> In Eden Adam sinned; in Gethsemane the Saviour
>   overcame sin.
> In Eden Adam fell; in Gethsemane Jesus conquered.
> In Eden Adam hid himself, in Gethsemane our
>   Lord boldly presented Himself.
> In Eden the sword was drawn; in Gethsemane
>   it was sheathed.

There is a strong poetic imagery even in the physical surroundings of moving toward the Garden of Gethsemane. John writes that Jesus "went forth with His disciples over the ravine of the Kidron" (John 18:1). A drain ran from the temple altar down to the Kidron ravine to take away the blood of sacrifice. Since it was the Passover, more than 200,000 lambs would be slain in the next day. When Jesus and His band crossed the Kidron, it was red with the blood of the lambs prepared for sacrifice. Within a few hours, the blood of the Lamb of God would flow.

His Agony

We see Jesus' lordship in relation to the agony that was before Him. Because John did not write much about Christ's anticipation of the Cross, there is a considerable gap between verses 1 and 2, which can be filled in by the accounts in the other Gospels. There we see a picture of protracted agony, of an unspeakable horror which came over Christ in Gethsemane as He wrestled with the reality of what was to come.

Matthew records that He "began to be grieved and distressed. Then He said to them, 'My soul is deeply grieved, to the point of death' " (26:37-38).

Mark tells us that Christ repeatedly fell to the ground, as He prayed that if it were possible, the hour might pass Him by (14:35). He evidently was in such agony that He would cast Himself to the ground and then stand up, and then fall again to the ground in prayer.

Luke, the physician, wrote: "And being in agony He was praying very fervently; and His sweat became like drops of blood, falling down upon the ground" (22:44). As the approaching dread engulfed Him, He actually broke out in a bloody sweat.

Verses such as these have caused some heretics in the church to argue that Christ was only a man, that He displayed less fortitude in the Garden and on the Cross than other men have shown in battle or at the stake.

Yet Christ's agony demonstrates that He knew exactly what was before Him. The approaching pain didn't cause His horror. Nor was it the shame of crucifixion, nor the desertion of His friends. His agony was caused by the fact that He was going to drink our cup, that He was going to pay the penalty for our sins.

Christ's resolve to endure the agony, even at such a price, was a demonstration of His lordship and His divinity.

Jesus prayed three times for the cup to be removed from Him. And after each time of prayer He found the disciples asleep. During this extended time of prayer, angels came and ministered to Him, so that He was strengthened to go on in prayer. John takes up the account after Jesus had finished His third session of prayer and had wakened the disciples to ready themselves to meet His captors.

> Now Judas also, who was betraying Him, knew the place; for Jesus had often met there with His disciples. Judas then, having received the Roman cohort, and officers from the chief priests and the Pharisees, came there with lanterns and torches and weapons (18:2-3).

It was the middle of a spring night. The moon was full and the sky was probably cloudless, for John mentioned that it was cold. The ancient olive trees cast eerie shadows across the encampment. Beyond the ravine lay the scattered lights of Jerusalem, where Judas had earlier made his rendezvous with the Roman cohort of 600 men from the Tower of Antonia. Matthew called that cohort a "great multitude" (26:47). The soldiers were armed, each carrying a short sword. With them came temple guards with their clubs. Jews and Gentiles were united in a common cause against Jesus.

The captors had carefully chosen the time and place, for they wanted to arrest Jesus away from the people, so that there would be no rioting. As Jesus and the disciples watched the approach of the soldiers, they would have seen a long line of flickering torches winding down from the dark and high walls of the Holy City, across the stained Kidron, up the slopes of Olivet. No doubt Judas was at the head of the procession, for it was planned that He would kiss Jesus so that the soldiers would know which man they were after.

H. G. Wells once said that the world is like a great stage play, produced and managed by God. As the curtain rises, the set is perfect, the characters are resplendent. Everything goes well until the leading man steps on the hem of the leading lady's gown, causing her to trip over a chair which knocks over a lamp which pushes over a table. The table falls into a side wall which knocks over the scenery. Finally, everything falls down on the heads of the actors. Behind the scenes, God, the producer, is running around, shouting orders, pulling strings, trying desperately to restore order from chaos. But, alas, He is unable to do so (D. James Kennedy, *Truths That Transform*, Fleming H. Revell, p. 16).

To the unbelieving eye, Jesus' arrest might appear to be controlled totally by His enemies; and yet as we now see Jesus with His antagonists, we know this is not true.

His Antagonists

Jesus therefore, knowing all the things that were coming upon Him, went forth, and said to them, "Whom do you seek?" They answered Him, "Jesus the Nazarene." He said to them, "I am He." And Judas also who was betraying Him, was standing with them. When therefore He said to them, "I am He," they drew back, and fell to the ground (18:4-6).

Instead of waiting to be found, Jesus went forward to meet the cohort. In response to their questions, He identified Himself. Their response was to fall to the ground. The grammatical construction presents their action as a miracle. Notice that they didn't fall when He asked them what they wanted. Nor did they fall merely because of the moral force that some great and good people possess. They knew nothing of Jesus and had no reason to fear Him.

They fell to the ground only after He said to them, "I am He," or literally, "I AM." Jesus answered them as Deity, using the divine predicate "I AM" that reaches back to God's encounter with Moses at the burning bush when God said, "I AM WHO I AM" (Ex. 3:13-14).

Jesus' answer was one of His last uses of the power by which

He calmed the seas, stilled the winds, and healed the sick. The cohort didn't arrest Jesus—He arrested them. His words were a gracious warning that they were in over their heads. Christ was not caught on the wheel of history. Rather, He is the axis of history.

> Again therefore He asked them, "Whom do you seek?" And they said, "Jesus the Nazarene." Jesus answered, "I told you that I am He; if therefore you seek Me, let these go their way," that the word might be fulfilled which He spoke, "Of those whom Thou hast given Me I lost not one" (18:7-9).

There can be little doubt but that the soldiers had intended to arrest the entire band. Luther believed that Christ's protection of His followers was the greatest miracle of all that occurred in Gethsemane. Jesus' method was obvious. Twice He asked the cohort whom they were looking for and twice they verbalized, "Jesus the Nazarene." The effect of this was to narrow their psychological focus. The end result was that His suggestion—that His followers be let go—seemed quite reasonable.

His Purpose

> Simon Peter therefore having a sword, drew it, and struck the high priest's slave, and cut off his right ear; and the slave's name was Malchus. Jesus therefore said to Peter, "Put the sword into the sheath; the cup which the Father has given Me, shall I not drink it?" (18:10-11)

I personally believe that this is the moment when Judas kissed Jesus, and that the whole effect was too much for Peter. Out came his hidden short sword as he lunged at Malchus. His sword came down hard on Malchus' helmet and, bounding down the right side, lopped off his right ear. Our primal instincts thrill that at least one blow was struck for Jesus. "It's just You and me, Jesus. Run for it, men. I'll meet you at the Jordan!"

The sobering truth is that Peter's action could have destroyed the church that was about to come into being. Calvin comments on this: "No thanks to him that Christ was not kept from death and that His name was not a perpetual disgrace" (John Calvin, *The Gospel According to St. John 11—21* and *The First Epistle of John,* Wm. B. Eerdmans, p. 156).

Imagine the scene as 600 steel blades rang from their scabbards, as Malchus touched the place where his ear had been and felt the steaming blood pouring through his fingers. Then came Jesus' words: "Stop! No more of this" (Luke 22:51). He touched Malchus' ear and healed him.

Even in His final moments, our Lord was merciful. But more than that, He was riveted to His purpose: "The cup which the Father has given Me, shall I not drink it?" (18:11) His cup was the cross. It was the cup of judgment that we should rightly have had to drink, and yet Jesus took it for us.

> Death and the curse were in that cup,
> O Christ, 'twas full for Thee;
> But Thou hast drained the last dark dregs,
> 'Tis empty now for me.

Jesus had wrestled with the terror of the cup, as He prayed, "Not my will, but Thine be done." Now He sovereignly said, "Shall I not drink it?"

How does all this relate to us? Although Christ's Gethsemane was infinitely beyond our human experience, our lesser Gethsemanes are a part of life. All of us have times of great stress in which the cup seems too much to drink. We all know what it feels like to be caught on the merciless wheel of life, with no control over what is happening to us.

Just as Christ governed His own destiny, even when it seemed to be out of control, so He can bring this control factor into our experience.

Joseph found this out, after he was sold into slavery by his brothers, then promoted, then demoted because of his righteousness, sent to jail, disappointed by his friends, forgotten, alone, and then suddenly raised to a position of great prominence. In retrospect, anyone can see God at work. But in the process, who knew God's hand was present, except Joseph? God is in control, even in the darkest hour. While men may intend evil, God intends good (Gen. 50:20).

> All those who journey, soon or late,
> Must pass within the garden's gate;
> Must kneel alone in darkness there,
> And battle with some fierce despair.
> God pity those who cannot say,
> "not mine but thine," who only pray,
> "Let this cup pass," and cannot see
> The *purpose* in Gethsemane.
> ("Gethsemane" in *Poems of Power*,
> E. W. Wilcox, quoted from C. E. Macartney's
> *Great Nights of the Bible*,
> Abingdon-Cokesbury, p. 166)

Gethsemane was not an ultimate tragedy. Neither are our Gethsemanes. I am not minimizing the pain of human loss and injustice. Yet behind what we call tragedy stands the wise purpose of the Lord of human history. Life is dark at times, the world seems to be falling apart, the wheel appears about to crush us. But this is not the end. For we know that God causes everything to work together for good in the lives of those who love Him, who are called according to His purpose—even in Gethsemane.

16
Pilate Before Jesus
John 18:24-40

In 1981 I was in Asia as a guest of the World Relief Commission, to see its refugee work in Hong Kong, Thailand, and the Philippines. As we arrived in Manila from Bangkok, we were informed that we would have to remain on the plane for an hour because our arrival conflicted with the arrival of the Prime Minister of Sri Lanka. As our plane taxied to a stop, I saw a scene that was particularly striking in contrast with the refugee camps I had just been in.

In formation on the runway were several hundred official welcomers, along with President and Mrs. Marcos. A platoon of honor guards wore shining gold pith helmets. Next to them was another platoon dressed in forest green and mustard, with white gloves and hats. There was a band uniformed in crimson and gold, dancers in chartreuse and purple, a baby elephant clad in scarlet. A long red carpet led to the Prime Minister's jet which had just landed bearing the words, "Hurray for Hollywood." Next came a 21-gun salute, then a procession of black stretch limos.

So much preparation and pomp, and yet after a few words, some ringing volleys, everyone was gone. It seemed a parable of earthly power—a big show, lots of noise, the world in obeisance. And then in an instant, the spectacle is gone.

In his poem "Ozymandias," Shelley tells of a traveler crossing the desert and finding a monument in the sand.

> I met a traveler from an antique land
> Who said: "Two vast and trunkless legs of stone
> Stand in the desert. Near them, on the sand,
> Half sunk, a shattered visage lies, whose frown,
> And wrinkled lip, and sneer of cold command,
> Tell that its sculptor well those passions read
> Which yet survive, stamped on these lifeless things,
> The hand that mocked them, and the heart that fed;
> And on the pedestal these words appear:
> 'My name is Ozymandias, king of kings:
> Look on my works, ye Mighty, and despair!'
> Nothing beside remains. Round the decay
> Of that colossal wreck, boundless and bare,
> The lone and level sands stretch far away."
> (*The Poetical Works of Shelley*,
> Houghton Mifflin, p. 366)

Earthly kingdoms, no matter how impressive, are ephemeral.
They prove that life is often not what it seems to be. We saw
this in connection with the arrest of Jesus, as He was actually
in control of the situation. We now see the same reversal as
Jesus is brought before Pilate.

Pilate's Pedigree

Pilate was an ambitious opportunist who, as procurator of Judea,
had gotten himself in over his head. He was brutal, politically
inept, and anti-semitic. He was a native of Seville, Spain who
had joined the Roman Legions and then married Claudia Procula,
a granddaughter of the Emperor Augustus. His administration
of Judea was noted for political mistakes which revealed severe
character flaws. For instance, on his initial visit to Jerusalem,
he enraged the Jews by having his soldiers carry banners embla-
zoned with the image of Tiberias. His manner of dealing with
ensuing protests was savage and impolitic.

On another occasion, he foolishly had his soldiers raid the sacred "Corban" treasury of the temple for funds to build an aqueduct. When the citizenry objected, he attacked the demonstrators. Later, he incensed the populace by having votive shields bearing Tiberias' image placed in Herod's palace. Luke mentions that he mingled the blood of certain Galileans with their sacrifices. They were evidently attacked while they were worshiping.

This remarkable series of incidents had not left Pilate in the good graces of Rome. He was not the typical efficient Roman administrator and, consequently, was suffering from job insecurity. He was probably under investigation, and evidence seems to indicate that he committed suicide a few years later in Gaul.

For a man of Pilate's background, judging Jesus' case should have been a simple matter, but it wasn't. The Jews wanted Him dead, but they wouldn't do the deed because it was unlawful for them (John 18:31).

Caiaphas, the high priest, wanted Him dead, and by crucifixion, so that He would be displayed before the people as cursed. Caiaphas thought that if Jesus were crucified, the Jews would look at Him and say, "He cannot be the Blessed One." Caiaphas was thinking of the Old Testament Scripture which said that anyone who was hanged on a tree was accursed of God (Deut. 21:22-23). He either didn't know or didn't care that Jesus had predicted His mode of death: "As Moses lifted up the serpent in the wilderness, even so must the Son of man be lifted up" (John 3:14).

While Pilate was holding court, his wife sent him a message asking that he have nothing to do with Jesus whom she called "the righteous Man" (Matt. 27:19).

Frank Morison in his book, *Who Moved the Stone?*, theorizes that Pilate and Claudia were probably spending the night together on the evening Jesus was arrested and that Claudia would, therefore, have known of the visit and purpose of Caiaphas' delegation to Pilate. The result was that as she went to bed her thoughts were quite naturally on Jesus—and so her dream. When she woke in the morning and found that Pilate had already left the palace, she at once guessed his business—so she quickly wrote the warning message which Matthew records (London: Faber and Faber, Limited, 1959, pp. 47—53)

The message from his wife left Pilate torn between the call of two worlds, the material world of advantage and the spiritual world of truth.

Jesus' Confession

When Pilate entered the Praetorium and summoned Jesus to him, he asked, "You are the King of the Jews?" (18:33) In all four Gospels, the word *You* is emphatic. Although Pilate was asking a legal question, he was first of all rendering an incredulous exclamation. "Are *You* the King of the Jews— *You?*" It was no wonder that Pilate reacted that way. Jesus was in peasant dress that was stained with bloody sweat from Gethsemane. His features were probably swollen from the agony.

Jesus turned the tables on Pilate, "Are you saying this on your own initiative, or did others tell you about Me?" (18:34) "What about you, Pilate?" Jesus was after Pilate's heart. And Pilate was on trial.

He blustered contemptuously, "I am not a Jew, am I? Your own nation and the chief priests delivered You up to me; what have You done?" (18:35)

Pilate's smokescreen was ineffective and Jesus came to the heart of the matter.

> Jesus answered, "My kingdom is not of this world. If My kingdom were of this world, then My servants would be fighting, that I might *not* be delivered up to the Jews; but as it is, My kingdom is not of this realm" (18:36).

Jesus had proclaimed Himself a spiritual king. Such a king does not rule by material force. His reply threw Pilate into a quandary. If Jesus had proclaimed Himself an earthly king, Pilate's decision would have been so easy, Claudia's dream would have proven wrong, and death would have been an easy sentence to pronounce. But a spiritual king? Politically, Jesus was guilty of nothing.

As Jesus stood before Pilate, He was in stark contrast to the Pilates of this world.

Jesus gave up His glory. Pilates will do anything to receive power, honor, and glory.

Jesus lived and taught that we are not to lay up for ourselves riches on this earth. Pilates value only what they can touch, taste, and feel.

Jesus mourned, "You seek Me, not because you saw signs, but because you ate of the loaves, and were filled" (John 6:26). Pilates rule by material manipulation.

Jesus had "no beauty that we should know Him" (Isa. 53). Pilates are arrayed in royal garments.

> Pilate therefore said to Him, "So You are a king?" Jesus answered, "You say correctly that I am a King. For this I have been born, and for this I have come into the world, to bear witness to the truth. Every one who is of the truth hears My voice" (18:37).

Christ was born to establish a new kind of kingdom. He cried, "For this I have been born!" Everyone who is of the truth knows that there is a spiritual kingdom and seeks it and hears the voice of the Saviour. Christ calls a materialistic world to seek first the kingdom of God.

Pilate's Confession

"Pilate said to Him, 'What is truth?' " (18:38). It is important to grasp the tone of his words. Francis Bacon thought that Pilate spoke in jest: " 'What is truth?' said jesting Pilate, and would not stay for an answer." Pilate was not joking. He was sarcastic, perhaps, but confused and despairing. He was a materialist, hungrily pursuing fantasies of power, fame, and satisfaction. Yet in that moment, he was arrested by his wife's spiritual premonition and by the mystical authority of Christ. Yet we do know that he didn't want an answer, because he didn't wait for one.

Convinced of Jesus' innocence, Pilate did his best to escape responsibility. The other Gospels tell us that he sent Jesus to Herod when he realized that Jesus was a Galilean. He hoped that Herod would see the trial as his jurisdictional responsibility. But when Jesus would not perform any tricks for Herod, the cruel king dressed Christ in a gorgeous robe, had Him beaten, and sent Him back to Pilate.

Barabbas' Substitute

Pilate was discouraged at Herod's return of Jesus until he remembered a Jewish tradition that seemed to offer a solution. At Passover the people were permitted to ask for the liberation of one prisoner. This symbolic act was in remembrance of God's mercy in delivering the Israelites from the bondage of Egypt. Pilate thought that if he offered a choice between Jesus and Barabbas, Jesus would go free.

Barabbas was a robber, an insurrectionist, and a murderer (John 18:40; Mark 15:7; Luke 23:19). Matthew called him a "notorious prisoner" (27:16). Pilate could not imagine that the people would choose to free such a criminal.

But as we know, the crowd chose Barabbas. Pilate was obviously very surprised at the crowd's choice. And what about Barabbas? The Praetorium was no more than 1,500 feet from the Tower of Antonia where Barabbas was incarcerated, awaiting crucifixion. He probably couldn't hear Pilate speak to the crowd, but it would have been impossible not to hear the roar of the crowd.

In Matthew 27 we find the dialogue between Pilate and the crowd about Barabbas. What Barabbas would have heard from the crowd was this: "Barabbas!"

"Crucify Him. Crucify Him."

"His blood be upon us and our children!" (vv. 21-25)

Hardened as he was, Barabbas must have grown faint. He may have stared at the palms of his hands in growing horror of the awaiting agony. He had seen crucifixions and knew of the interminable suffering involved.

And then he heard the sound of the key in the lock and found himself released from his chains, a free man. As he emerged into the sunlight, he gradually learned that someone named Jesus had taken his place.

> Barabbas was the only man in the world who could say that Jesus Christ took his physical place. But I can say that Jesus Christ took my spiritual place. For it was I who deserved to die. It was I who deserved that the wrath of God should be poured upon me. I deserved the eternal punishment of the lake of fire. He was delivered up for my offenses. He was handed over to judgment because of my sins. This is why we speak of the substitutionary atonement. Christ was my substitute. He was satisfying the debt of divine justice and holiness. That is why I say that Christianity can be expressed in the three phrases: I deserved hell; Jesus took my hell; there is nothing left for me but His heaven (Donald Grey Barnhouse, *Romans,* vol. 2 "God's Remedy," Fincastle, Virginia: Scripture Truth Book Co., p. 378).

> He made Him who knew no sin to be sin on our behalf, that we might become the righteousness of God in Him (2 Cor. 5:21).

> And He Himself bore our sins in His body on the cross, that we might die to sin and live to righteousness; for by His wounds you were healed (1 Peter 2:24).

Jesus died in place of all those who respond to Him. He reversed the sentence of His people in Pilate's judgment hall. How about you? Has He reversed your sentence? Have you said, "Not any other but this man, Christ"?

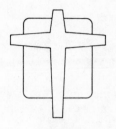

17

"Behold, the Man!"

John 19:1-16

In the introduction to a Greek play is the Latin phrase, *dramatis personae,* which means "people of the drama." Under this are listed the choruses, characters, or groups of people in the play.

As our story of Christ's trial continues, we find ourselves facing a dramatis personae that would have made a Greek playwright pale with envy.

The religious leaders are so blinded by their hatred for Jesus that they do not see the deathly inconsistency of their own lives. They are so scrupulous about the smallest religious details that they will not defile themselves by even entering Pilate's residence. Yet they are unified and intent on trapping Pilate into performing a judicial murder.

Also on the list is Pontius Pilate, representative of Imperial Rome, the greatest power on earth. Pilate is a man to whom success means everything.

And then there is Jesus, of whom mere description can never do justice.

The underlying theme of this play is that life is not what it seems to be on the surface. For even now, as He is on trial, it is not Christ who is caught on the wheel of history, but Pilate.

This act of the drama takes place inside the Praetorium and also on its portico. Scene One takes place inside the Praetorium where the Roman soldiers scourge and mock Jesus. Scene Two is outside on the portico where Pilate presents Jesus to the people. Scene Three moves back inside the Praetorium, where Pilate talks privately with Jesus about the matter of authority. Scene Four is out on the portico, where Christ is publicly delivered up for crucifixion.

Scene One: The Soldiers Mock Jesus

Pilate is disappointed because his attempts to escape responsibility for Jesus have failed. Herod has returned Christ to Pilate, refusing to take Him as his jurisdictional charge, and the crowd has called for the release of Barabbas over Jesus.

Now Pilate attempts another play. He informs the multitude that he will punish Jesus and then release Him (Luke 23:16).

> Then Pilate therefore took Jesus, and scourged Him. And the soldiers wove a crown of thorns and put it on His head, and arrayed Him in a purple robe; and they began to come up to Him and say, "Hail, King of the Jews!" and to give Him blows in the face (John 19:1-3).

Scourging was a terrible punishment. Many died from it and others went mad. Ancient authorities as diverse as Eusebius, Josephus, and Cicero relate that scourging normally meant a flaying to the bone. Eusebius tells of martyrs who "were torn by scourges down to deep-seated veins and arteries, so that the hidden contents of the recesses of their bodies, their entrails and organs were exposed to sight" (Eusebius, *The Ecclesiastical History iv 15, 4,* Translated by Kirsopp Lake, Harvard University Press, vol. 2., p. 341).

Because the Roman soldiers hated the Jews, they took an act of scourging a Jew as a way to show further contempt. Is Jesus the Jewish King? Then He will have a crown! So they plait a crown of thorns and set it on Christ's bleeding head.

The gruesome carnival continues as the soldiers array Him in a purple robe, probably using a soldier's ragged robe faded from crimson to purple. Matthew and Mark tell us that the soldiers make Christ hold a reed sceptre and then repeatedly take it from His hand and beat Him about the face.

Scene Two: Pilate Presents Jesus

We move out into the light of the courtyard where Pilate is about to make a bid for Jesus' freedom.

> And Pilate came out again, and said to them, "Behold, I am bringing Him out to you, that you may know that I find no guilt in Him (19:4).

Then he presents to them Jesus, who is wearing the crown of thorns and the purple robe. The scourge has done its work. The flesh has been cut away from Christ's ribs as well as from his back. Some ribs are exposed. His appearance is "marred more than any man, and His form more than the sons of men" (Isa. 52:14).

The people stare and Pilate hopes they will feel not only revulsion but some sympathy. And so Pilate shouts, "Behold, the Man!" (19:5) His cry rings out through eternity. The literal meaning of his cry is "Poor man!" or "Poor creature!" He is in effect asking, "Haven't you hounded Him enough?"

Yet in saying, "Behold, the Man!" Pilate is affirming more than he ever will know. This is a call to reflect on the Incarnation. *The Man* is standing before the people. God has become a Man and this is what He looks like. We are asked to behold this Man.

The form and visage of Jesus is a drawing of love. To see how much God loves us, we watch Christ through the course of the Cross. We listen to His cry as He is bearing our sins: "My God, My God, why hast Thou forsaken Me?" (Matt. 27:46; Ps. 22:1)

Pilate realizes that he has aroused no sympathy for Jesus. For the leaders of the people, the chief priest, and the officers cry out, "Crucify, crucify!" Pilate says to them, "Take Him yourselves, and crucify Him, for I find no guilt in Him" (19:6).

Three times Pilate has judged Christ not guilty. In so doing, he has heaped eternal damnation on himself as well as on the multitude. The leaders of the people come back with one more argument:

> "We have a law, and by that law He ought to die because He made Himself out to be the Son of God" (19:7).

When Pilate hears this and begins to understand the nature of Jesus' offense against the Jews, he pulls Him back into the recesses of the Praetorium, to attempt to talk with Him.

Scene Three: Pilate Talks with Jesus

In this intimate conversation, we see that the prisoner and the free man are one—Jesus Christ. He controls the conversation, notably by His use of silence. Pilate asks Him, "Where are You from?" (19:9) And Jesus does not answer. Mark and Luke describe His silence as so pronounced that it provokes Pilate's telling question and Jesus' supreme reply:

> Pilate therefore said to Him, "You do not speak to me? Do You not know that I have authority to release You, and I have authority to crucify You?" Jesus answered, "You would have no authority over Me, unless it had been given you from above; for this reason he who delivered Me up to you has the greater sin" (19:10-11).

Pilate, who wants so much to release Jesus, cannot do so. He is bound by his own ambitions, by the system in which he works. He looks with awe at this battered but free Man who stands before him.

As if they sense Pilate's desire to try again to release Jesus, the people call out to him to remind him of his fragile connection with Caesar, and of the possibility that he can be replaced.

> As a result of this Pilate made efforts to release Him, but the Jews cried out, saying, "If you release this Man, you are no friend of Caesar" (19:12).

Scene Four: Pilate Yields to the Jews

When Pilate hears what the people are saying to him, he leads Jesus outside again and seats himself at the judgment seat "at a place called The Pavement, but in Hebrew, *Gabbatha*" (19:13).

Pilate is giving up. Even though he knows Christ is innocent, even though he has heard hints of divinity, despite Claudia's warning to have nothing to do with this righteous Man, and though he is frantic to see Christ released, he can do nothing now but back off. Pilate's heart is set on power, position, money, celebrity, and he is captive to his choices.

This act concludes as Pilate yields to the people. He sits at the judgment seat watching the crowds, listening to their demands. When there is a lull in the shouting, he says to the people, "Behold, your King!" (19:14)

Just as this is taking place, the priests are beginning to slaughter the Passover lambs in the temple. The Lamb of God has timed His sacrifice to coincide with the sacrificing of the paschal lambs. He is the King.

We spoke of the *dramatis personae* in this drama. And yet as the act closes, there is only One who draws our full attention. "Behold, the Man. . . . Behold, your King!"

18
The Sin-Bearer
John 19:17-30

The late Dr. Donald Grey Barnhouse told of a Saturday morning when he was in his study working. The custodian came in and announced that a man was waiting outside to see him. He gave Dr. Barnhouse the man's card which indicated that he was the captain of the *Mauritania,* the largest passenger vessel crossing the Atlantic.

As Dr. Barnhouse went out to meet his visitor, the captain said, "You have a very beautiful church here."

Dr. Barnhouse replied, "We are grateful for all that was done by our faithful predecessors 100 years ago to provide us with these facilities."

As they walked through the church, the captain said, "It is very much like the Basilica at Ravenna in Italy."

Dr. Barnhouse answered, "Well, it is an architectural duplication. In fact, years ago the tessellated ceilings and the marble columns and the mosaic were all done by Italian workmen. But that's not what you came to talk about, is it?"

The captain replied, "No. Twenty-three times a year, I sail the Atlantic. When I come down the bank of Newfoundland, I hear your broadcast out of Boston. And as I came in this week, I thought to myself, 'I've got twenty-four hours in New York. I'm going to get down and see Dr. Barnhouse.' So I took a train, hoping perhaps I would be able to meet you, and here I am."

Dr. Barnhouse was very straightforward with the captain as he asked, "Sir, have you been born again?"

"That is what I came to see you about."

By that time they had reached a chalkboard in the prayer room and Dr. Barnhouse drew three crosses on the board. Underneath the first one he wrote the word IN. Underneath the third he wrote the word IN. Underneath the middle cross he wrote the words NOT IN. Then he said to the captain, "Do you understand what I mean when I say that the two men who died with Jesus had sin IN them?"

The captain thought and then said, "Yes, I do. Christ did not have sin within Him."

Then over the first cross and over the third, Dr. Barnhouse wrote the word ON. He said, "Do you understand what that means?" The captain wrinkled his brow—he didn't quite understand.

Dr. Barnhouse said, "Let me illustrate. Have you ever run through a red light?"

"Yes," the captain replied.

"Were you caught?"

"No."

"Well, in running that red light, you had sin IN you. If you had been caught, you would have had sin ON you. So here the thieves bore the penalty of God." Then he wrote ON over the middle cross and said, "Jesus bore your sins. There was no sin IN Him, but the sin was laid ON HIM." Then he crossed out the ON over the first thief and drew an arrow over to Christ and said, "His sins rested on Christ by virtue of his faith—belief in Christ." And then Dr. Barnhouse asked the captain, "Which one of the two are you?"

The captain was a tall, distinguished looking man, and as he stood there deciding, Dr. Barnhouse could see that he was moved, for he was fighting back the tears as he said, "By the grace of God, I am the first man."

Dr. Barnhouse answered, "You mean your sins are on Jesus?"

"Yes, God says my sins are on Jesus." He shot out his hand and said, "That's what I came to find out."

Dr. Barnhouse invited him to lunch and further shared the Gospel with him. And the captain went back to New York a new believer in Christ (Donald Grey Barnhouse, *The Love Life,* Regal, pp. 270-273).

In Christ's crucifixion on the cross, we each can see this same diagram of love. Let us look at some of the details of that awful day.

Lamb of God

> They took Jesus therefore; and He went out, bearing His own cross, to the place called the Place of a Skull, which is called in Hebrew, Golgotha; where they crucified Him, and with Him two other men, one on either side, and Jesus in between (John 19:17-18).

The Gospels tell us little about Jesus' pitiful route to the cross; such processions were as common as funeral marches. Yet we have some details from history. Jesus was placed in the center of a quarternion, a company of four Roman soldiers. The crossbeam or patibulum of the cross was placed on His torn shoulders like an oar. This weighed over 100 pounds. As Christ stumbled along the route to Calvary, an officer preceded Him carrying a placard describing Jesus' crime. It read, "Jesus the Nazarene, the King of the Jews." Customarily, a man about to be crucified was led to the site of his execution by the longest route possible, so that everyone might see that "crime does not pay" and also to give opportunity to anyone who might speak up in his defense. So it was that Christ trod the Via Dolorosa so weakened, finally, that a bystander had to be drafted to carry the cross the rest of the way.

At the place of the execution, Christ was laid upon the patibulum. Spikes were driven through His hands or wrists and then the crossbar was hoisted into place. His legs were nailed, leaving only enough flex in the knees so that He could begin the horrible up-and-down motion necessary for breathing. The medical assessments of the rhythmic misery provide a terrible picture.

But this physical pain was just a shadow of the agony Christ would experience when our sins were poured on Him and He entered the greater horror of separation from His Father.

John tells of the thieves on either side of Him: "They crucified Him, and with Him two other men, one on either side, and Jesus in between" (19:18). If the cross is a diagram of His love, the positioning of the crosses is a diagram of how His love is dispensed to the world. The Lord's enemies intended the positioning of the crosses to be His final disgrace—Christ between two convicted robbers, as if He were the worst. Instead of being a disgrace, however, it was a fulfillment of Isaiah's prophecy, where it is said that Christ:

> was numbered with the transgressors; yet He Himself bore the sin of many, and interceded for the transgressors (Isa. 53:12).

King of the Jews

> And Pilate wrote an inscription also, and put it on the cross. And it was written, "JESUS THE NAZARENE, THE KING OF THE JEWS." Therefore this inscription many of the Jews read, for the place where Jesus was crucified was near the city; and it was written in Hebrew, Latin, and in Greek.
>
> And so the chief priests of the Jews were saying to Pilate, "Do not write, 'The King of the Jews'; but that He said, 'I am King of the Jews.' "
>
> Pilate answered, "What I have written I have written" (19:19-22).

Jesus' enemies didn't like Pilate's inscription, "Jesus the Nazarene, the King of the Jews." The use of the imperfect verb suggests that the Jews repeatedly asked Pilate to change the sign to read, "He said, 'I am King of the Jews.' " Pilate would not change it and answered in the finality of the perfect tense, "What I have written, I have written, and it will always remain written."

At Christ's birth, wise men from the east heralded Him as

King. At the beginning of the Passion Week, the multitudes had cried, "Blessed is the King of Israel." Before Pilate, Christ bore witness to His kingdom. Now His royal title was affixed to His very cross. Ultimately, He will come as King of kings and Lord of lords.

Son of Man

> The soldiers therefore, when they had crucified Jesus, took His outer garments and made four parts, a part to every soldier and also the tunic; now the tunic was seamless, woven in one piece. They said therefore to one another; "Let us not tear it, but cast lots for it, to decide whose it shall be"; that the Scripture might be fulfilled, "They divided My outer garments among them, and for My clothing they cast lots" (19:23-24).

Since every Jewish man wore five pieces of clothing—sandals, a turban, a belt, an inner tunic, and an outer robe—it is easy to surmise what happened to Jesus' garments. Each soldier chose one of the less expensive articles. Realizing that it would be foolish to divide the robe in four parts, they gambled for it. Ultimately they were fulfilling the prophecy of Psalm 22:18: "They divide My garments among them, and for My clothing they cast lots." It is one thing to take a dead man's belongings and quite another to gamble over them while the man is still dying and can see what is going on. This is life at its lowest. The four Roman soldiers are a capsulization of the world's neglect of the significance of Christ's atoning death.

A world without God is dramatically portrayed in Golding's *Lord of the Flies.* In the novel, British children are marooned on an island and there resort to a nightmare of murder. They are finally rescued by civilization in the form of a British warship which then continues on its way to hunt the enemy in the same implacable manner that the children had stooped to on the island. We live in a cold world where, too often, survival is for those who know "when to hold 'em and when to fold 'em."

Born of a Woman

Our text contains a contrast between the four soldiers and another group of four, a microcosm of those under Christ's care. Four women stood at the foot of the cross, "His mother, and His mother's sister, Mary the wife of Clopas, and Mary Magdalene" (19:25). The contrast with the soldiers points out Jesus' loving care and provision for His own.

It is difficult to imagine what was going on in the minds and hearts of the women, and especially His mother. She must have thought back over His whole life, to the moment of His birth and then eight days later when she and Joseph took Him to the temple to present Him to the Lord. And she remembered the words of the aged Simeon, as he prophesied by the Holy Spirit:

> Behold, this Child is appointed for the fall and rise of many in Israel, and for a sign to be opposed—and a sword will pierce even your own soul—to the end that thoughts from many hearts may be revealed (Luke 2:34-35).

There on the cross, Mary saw the baby she had held and nursed, this One who had brought only joy to her and to Joseph. And now the sword was piercing her heart.

His mother's sister was Salome, Zebedee's wife, the mother of James and John (Mark 15:40 and Matt. 27:56). She had been sharply rebuffed by Christ for her ambition for her sons, but she had seen love in that rebuke. Now, with her sister, she was experiencing this family grief.

We know nothing of Mary, the wife of Clopas, but we know much of Mary Magdalene. Seven devils had been cast out of her. Jesus described her as one who had sinned much and who also loved much. Mary was the woman who came to Jesus in the Pharisee's house, while He reclined at dinner. She washed His feet with her tears, wiped them with her hair, and then anointed them with costly perfume.

> When Jesus therefore saw His mother, and the disciple whom He loved standing nearby, He said to His mother, "Woman,

behold your son!" Then He said to the disciple, "Behold, your mother!" And from that hour the disciple took her into his own household (19:26-27).

Jesus was in limitless pain as He went through cycles of twisting, straining tendons like violin strings, experiencing joint-rending cramps and intermittent asphyxiation. He was lingering at the fringes of death. Within the next hour, darkness would cover Calvary as He, in cosmic battle, would bear the world's sins alone in the darkness. Yet even now He thought of His own. As He was about to die, they were all in His heart. And that is a comfort for us. As He cared for them in His agony, we can know that He cares for us now in His exaltation. We have a Saviour who loves us so deeply that when we are hurting, He comes to us and makes provision for us.

John was evidently the only disciple at the cross, and now he stood alongside Mary, supporting her. As R.C.H. Lenski wrote, "These two belonged together because these two were losing in Jesus' death more than the rest" (*Preaching on John*, Baker Book House, pp. 47-48).

As they gazed up in misery at the mutilated form of their greatest love, Christ summoned all His strength and gasped, "John, this is your mother; and Woman, this is your son." So it was that John took Mary to his home.

For John, Christ's provision for him came in the form of a responsibility. John still had his own mother to care for. We need to realize that Christ's care for us may come in the form of responsibilities or burdens. It is natural for us to think that the more we love God, the less He will ask of us and the lighter will be our burdens. This isn't so. In fact, if John hadn't been at the foot of the cross, he would never have received this responsibility.

The burden He gave to John was His perfect blessing for him. This is not to say that all the burdens we bear are because we have loved God so well. Many burdens are due to our own sin and stupidity. But it is true that unique responsibilities are placed on those who possess great love.

Jesus' words to Mary marked the beginning of a new relationship with her, as He addressed her as "Woman." She had to yield to a higher, holier bond as He became her Saviour. Mary and those with her at the cross found their comfort in their faith in His atoning work.

Victor over Sin

The other Gospels tell us that after Jesus gave His mother to John, darkness fell on the land from the sixth hour until the ninth. Why the darkness? It was to hide the agony of Christ as He became a curse for us. In Jewish thinking, to be cursed was to be separated from God, while to be blessed was to see the face of God (Num. 6:24). Jesus had never known anything but the face of the Father. And now He became a curse as He bore our sins.

> For as many as are of the works of the Law are under a curse; for it is written, "Cursed is every one who does not abide by all things written in the Book of the Law, to perform them...." Christ redeemed us from the curse of the Law, having become a curse for us—for it is written, "Cursed is every one who hangs on a tree" (Gal. 3:10, 13).

At the moment of separation, the pain from the nails was as nothing to Jesus. He may not even have been aware of the physical pain, for there is nothing as painful as separation from God. Jesus cried out in the darkness, "My God, My God, why hast Thou forsaken Me?"

> After this, Jesus, knowing that all things had already been accomplished, in order that the Scripture might be fulfilled, said, "I am thirsty." A jar full of sour wine was standing there; so they put a sponge full of the sour wine upon a branch of hyssop, and brought it up to His mouth. When Jesus therefore had received the sour wine, He said, "It is finished!" And He bowed His head, and gave up His spirit (19:28-30).

As Christ spoke of His thirst, He fulfilled the words of Psalm 69:21, "And for My thirst they gave Me vinegar to drink." Even the unusual use of a branch of hyssop to extend the sponge to Christ's lips suggests scriptural parallels, because hyssop was the plant the Children of Israel used to apply the blood of the Passover lambs to the doorposts so that the death angel might pass over them (Ex. 12:22).

By this time, the body of Jesus was in extremis. He could feel the chill of death creeping through His tissues. With the greatest effort He pulled Himself up and shouted, "It is finished!" Then He bowed His head and gave up His spirit to God.

This was not a submissive cry but a shout of victory. In the Greek it is expressed in one word. Jesus used the perfect tense of the verb which means, "It is finished and always will be finished." What had He finished? The Law, the Old Testament types, the prophecies, and the complete atonement.

> Lifted up was He to die,
> "It is finished" was His cry. . . .
> Full atonement! Can it be?
> Hallelujah! What a Saviour!
> (P.P. Bliss)

His cry of victory came because He had done it all. "He made Him who knew no sin to be sin on our behalf, that we might become the righteousness of God in Him"(2 Cor. 5:21). He became a curse for us, so that we might never need to know the horror of separation from God. Not the most awful man who has ever lived has known complete separation from God, while in this world. Even the most sinful is surrounded by common grace. But Jesus experienced separation. And once it was in the past, He cried out with triumph, "It is finished!"

His finished work of redemption is the reason we must come to Him empty-handed. To think that we can commend ourselves to Christ with some work or ability of our own is to commit the infinite insult against God. We must come like the thief who hung beside Him on the cross:

> Nothing in my hand I bring,
> Simply to Thy cross I cling.

The ground of our comfort is that we will never be separated from God. Our prospect is fellowship with the Father and with the Son and the wonder of becoming more like Christ. As we behold His face as in a mirror, we will be constantly transformed into His likeness, and His face will shine on us.

Jesus' final words express the trust of His soul to His Father: "Father, into Thy hands I commit My spirit" (Luke 23:46).

Lord of All

As Christ finished His work on the cross, He was not only the suffering Saviour but also the conquering King. By virtue of His rule from the cross, Christ rightfully makes imperious demands on His followers. He demands that we yield to His lordship, which none of us does naturally. If it were not for the constant work of God's grace in us, we would assume the lordship of our own lives.

He demands that we each take up our cross and follow Him. When the people of Jesus' time heard Him say that they were to take up a cross, they understood this colloquial expression to mean that they were to die to themselves:

> Whoever does not carry his own cross and come after Me cannot be My disciple (Luke 14:27).

> If any one wishes to come after Me, let him deny himself, and take up his cross, and follow Me (Matt. 16:24).

> And he who does not take his cross and follow after Me is not worthy of Me (Matt. 10:38).

We must reject what Bonhoeffer called "cheap grace" as unworthy of the total self-giving of our Lord. Bonhoeffer described cheap grace:

The preaching of forgiveness without requiring repentance, baptism without church discipline, Communion without confession, absolution without personal confession. Cheap grace is grace without discipleship, grace without the cross, grace without Jesus Christ.

In contrast to this, he describes authentic grace as infinitely costly:

It is costly because it costs a man his life, and it is grace because it gives a man the only true life. . . . Above all, it is *costly* because it cost God the life of His Son: "Ye were bought at a price," and what has cost God much cannot be cheap for us. Above all, it is *grace* because God did not reckon His Son too dear a price to pay for our life, but delivered Him up for us (Dietrich Bonhoeffer, *The Cost of Discipleship,* Macmillan, pp. 47-48).

The cross is truly the diagram of God's love. As its benefits are infinite and eternal, so its demands are expansive:

> Love so amazing, so divine,
> demands my soul, my life, my all.

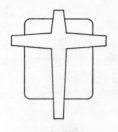

19
Resurrection Day
John 21:1-31

The unthinkable had happened. Christ was dead! The disciples had never believed it would end like this. Now there was no mental escape from their helplessness and their sense of shame.
Matthew tells what happened after Christ died:

> And behold, the veil of the temple was torn in two from top to bottom, and the earth shook; and the rocks were split, and the tombs were opened.... Now the centurion, and those who were with him keeping guard over Jesus, when they saw the earthquake and the things that were happening, became very frightened and said, "Truly this was the Son of God!" (Matt. 27:51-54)

Joseph of Arimathea, a secret disciple of Jesus, gained permission to bury Jesus' body. With the help of Nicodemus, he swaddled Jesus with linen wrappings and about 180 pounds of spices and then laid Him in a new garden tomb. Jesus' body was in the tomb until sometime before dawn on Sunday morning.

Discovering the Empty Tomb
Very early that Sunday morning, several women walked from the city to the tomb to anoint Christ's body with spices. Mat-

thew mentions Mary Magdalene and Mary, the mother of Jesus. Mark tells us that Salome was present. Luke includes Joanna.

These devoted women reached the tomb about daybreak in a light that made it difficult to see clearly. Yet what they could see shook them—the stone had been removed from the entrance to the tomb. Imagine their confusion—had someone broken into the tomb? Had Joseph and Nicodemus decided to move the body? Where were the soldiers?

As they talked about what they were seeing, the women decided that they needed to tell the disciples. And so Mary Magdalene, perhaps the youngest of the group, went to find the men. She located Peter and John and said:

> "They have taken away the Lord out of the tomb, and we do not know where they have laid Him."
>
> Peter therefore went forth, and the other disciple, and they were going to the tomb. And the two were running together; and the other disciple ran ahead faster than Peter, and came to the tomb first; and stooping and looking in, he saw the linen wrappings lying there; but he did not go in.
>
> Simon Peter therefore also came, following him, and entered the tomb; and he beheld the linen wrappings lying there, and the face-cloth, which had been on His head, not lying with the linen wrappings, but rolled up in a place by itself.
>
> Then entered in therefore the other disciple also, who had first come to the tomb, and he saw, and believed. For as yet they did not understand the Scripture, that He must rise again from the dead (John 20:2-9).

The Apostle John saw and believed, not merely that Jesus was gone, but that He was alive. Why did John believe? Because of something he saw in the tomb. The burial practices of the Jews were distinctive. The Egyptians embalmed their dead. The Romans and Greeks often cremated their dead. In Palestine neither was done. Rather, the dead were wrapped in linen swaddling containing dry spices and were laid on their backs in tombs. But they were not completely wrapped. The head, neck, and upper part of the shoulders were left bare. The head was wrapped separately, with a cloth twirled about it like a turban. This explains the action of the corpses come to life when Jesus raised the son of the widow of Nain and Lazarus (Luke 7:15; John 11:44). It also explains John's reaction at our Lord's tomb.

John reached the tomb first but he didn't go in. Rather, he stood looking at the linen wrappings. When Peter caught up, he brushed past John and entered the tomb, and also saw the linen wrappings. However, these men did not see in the same way. The word for see in John's case, *blepo,* suggests simple seeing. The word for Peter is *theoreo,* from which we get the word theater. Peter took a long careful look at "the linen wrappings lying there, and the face-cloth, which had been on His head, not lying with the linen wrappings, but rolled up in a place by itself" (20:6-7).

Peter saw the turban in place as it had been on Jesus. Then John entered the tomb and looked—*horao,* meaning to see with understanding—and he believed. He saw the undisturbed wrappings and the face cloth collapsed in the exact positions that they had covered Jesus' body and face, and he knew that Jesus was alive. John Stott says the body was vaporized as it became something wonderful and new (*Basic Christianity,* InterVarsity Press, p. 53). John realized that no one had done anything with the body. Jesus was risen.

Jesus is alive today, just as He was that morning. While we believe this, it is not always as real to us as it was to John and Peter that morning.

R.W. Dale was a British congregational minister and a distinguished leader in Christendom. Late in his life, while preparing an Easter sermon:

> The thought of the risen Lord broke in upon him as it had never done before. "Christ is alive," I said to myself; "alive!" and then I paused"—alive!" and then I paused again; "alive!" Can that really be true? Living as really as I myself am? I got up and walked about repeating, "Christ is living!" "Christ is living!"
> It was to me a new discovery. I thought that all along I had

believed it; but not until that moment did I feel sure about it. I then said, "My people shall know it; I shall preach about it again and again until they believe it as I do now." . . . Then began the custom of singing in Carr's Lane on every Sunday morning an Easter hymn (quoted by A. J. Gossip, *The Interpreter's Bible,* vol. 8, Abingdon, p. 792).

He is alive! If we can believe as Peter and John did, our lives will be changed. A living Christ is an all-powerful Christ. A living Christ is a present Christ. A living Christ gives us life now. He gives us life for eternity.

The Appearance of Jesus

While the two apostles believed, they hadn't seen Jesus. Mary Magdalene was to be the first to have that joy. When Peter and John sprinted to the tomb, after receiving Mary's message, they probably left her in the dust. And they were gone from the tomb when she got there.

Mary was standing outside the tomb, alone and uninformed and in tears. The Greek word indicates that she was sobbing and wailing in the typical eastern death wail. Jesus had cast seven devils from her. She had sinned much and had been forgiven much, and she loved Him accordingly. Now her heart was broken.

Mary was standing outside the tomb weeping; and so, as she wept, she stooped and looked into the tomb; and she beheld two angels in white sitting, one at the head, and one at the feet, where the body of Jesus had been lying. And they said to her, "Woman, why are you weeping?" She said to them, "Because they have taken away my Lord, and I do not know where they have laid Him" (20:11-13).

St. Chrysostom, in his commentary on this passage, suggests that one of the angels motioned for Mary to turn around.

When she had said this, she turned around, and beheld Jesus standing there, and did not know that it was Jesus. Jesus said to her, "Woman, why are you weeping? Whom are you seeking?"

Supposing Him to be the gardener, she said to Him, "Sir, if you have carried Him away, tell me where you have laid Him, and I will take Him away." Jesus said to her, "Mary!"

She turned and said to Him in Hebrew, "Rabboni!" (which means, Teacher).

Jesus said to her, "Stop clinging to Me; for I have not yet ascended to the Father; but go to My brethren, and say to them, "I ascend to My Father and your Father, and My God and your God" (20:14-17).

As Mary cried, "Rabboni," she threw her arms around Jesus. But He cautioned her. He wanted her to realize that a new relationship was in the process of being established. The comfort that awaited Mary and the other disciples was far more substantial than His physical presence could ever be.

It is highly significant that Christ appeared first to a woman and that this appearance is recorded by all four Gospels. It was not only to a woman, one who in that culture had been oppressed, but to a person who had known great sin. What a great comfort this should be to us. Christ always comes first to the poor in spirit. (See Matt. 5:3 and Luke 4:18.)

What Mary must have felt! She had been on an emotional roller coaster for days and now she was deliriously at the top. Off she went on another cross-country run to the disciples. This time she had more substantial news—she had seen Jesus!

What a day it had been. Multiple trips to the tomb, multiple retellings. The report of the encounter on the road to Emmaus. Dark threats and rumors too. By now, it was evening. Despite all their excitement, the apostolic band was afraid, and as they met together it was behind closed doors.

Suddenly, Jesus was in their midst and yet no one had opened the door. Their hearts raced; their adrenalin flowed. Then they heard His supreme greeting, "*Shalom*. Peace be with you" (20:19).

Jesus showed them His hands and side and "the disciples therefore rejoiced when they saw the Lord" (20:20). Luke adds that they "could not believe it for joy" (Luke 24:41).

Can anyone describe that night adequately? I think not. We reach the heights of mystery when we read:

> And when He had said this, He breathed on them, and said to them, "Receive the Holy Spirit. If you forgive the sins of any, their sins have been forgiven them; if you retain the sins of any, they have been retained" (20:22-23).

The Problem of Disbelief

On that most dramatic day in history, one disciple was missing. Thomas wasn't with the others. We all deal with our emotions differently, and perhaps Thomas' grief had driven him off by himself. He wasn't a coward for he was the one who had said, "Let us also go, that we may die with Him" (John 11:16). But for some reason he wasn't with the others when Jesus appeared. When they told him the news, he said:

> Unless I shall see in His hands the imprint of the nails, and put my finger into the place of the nails, and put my hand into His side, I will not believe (20:25).

Fortunately, there was a remedy for Thomas' unbelief and there is a remedy for us. The Lord gave Thomas time to think, one week to be exact. He may already have come to belief as he was with the other disciples, hearing them tell again and again their encounter with Jesus. And he was with them the next Sunday night.

> And after eight days again His disciples were inside, and Thomas with them. Jesus came, the doors having been shut, and stood in their midst, and said, "Peace be with you." Then He said to Thomas, "Reach here your finger, and see My hands; and reach here your hand, and put it into My side; and be not unbelieving, but believing." Thomas answered and said to Him, "My Lord and my God!" (20:26-28)

Thomas may have been slow to believe, but he was not slow to grasp the implications of Christ's resurrection. Jesus was not only his Lord but his God. His faith rested on solid rock.

But what about us? The evidence is still just as substantive, just as palpable as it was for Thomas. Jesus said to Thomas, "Because you have seen Me, have you believed? Blessed are they who did not see, and yet believed" (20:29). We can be part of that blessed company.

SEVEN STANZAS AT EASTER

Make no mistake: if He rose at all
it was as His body;
if the cells' dissolution did not reverse, the molecules
    reknit, the amino acids rekindle,
the Church will fall.

It was not as the flowers,
each soft Spring recurrent;
it was not as His Spirit in the mouths and fuddled
    eyes of the eleven apostles;
it was as His flesh: ours.

The same hinged thumbs and toes,
the same valved heart
that—pierced—died, withered, paused, and then
    regathered out of enduring Might
new strength to enclose.

Let us not mock God with metaphor,
analogy, sidestepping, transcendence;
making of the event a parable, a sign painted in the
    faded credulity of earlier ages:
let us walk through the door.

The stone is rolled back, not papier-mâché,
not a stone in a story,
but the vast rock of materiality that in the slow
    grinding of time will eclipse for each of us
the wide light of day.

And if we will have an angel at the tomb,
make it a real angel,
weighty with Max Planck's quanta, vivid with hair,
    opaque in the dawn light, robed in real linen
spun on a definite loom.

Let us not seek to make it less monstrous,
for our own convenience, our own sense of beauty,
lest, awakened in one unthinkable hour, we are
    embarrassed by the miracle,
and crushed by remonstrance.

                    JOHN UPDIKE

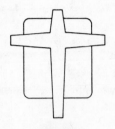

20
A Living Parable

John 21:1-14

John 21 is an epilogue to the Gospel of John. The opening event of this chapter, an all-night fishing expedition, is a living parable of how the risen Lord relates to His servants as they toil in the world. Of course, at the time the disciples had no idea that they were actors in a spiritual drama. But when it was over and as the days passed, giving opportunity for reflection, they knew.

Especially those who were fishermen knew, because of the parallels between that morning and the first time Jesus called them to be disciples. Both times there had been a frustrating night of fruitless toil. Jesus had commanded each time to let down the net once more. Each time there was an instant and great success. These parallels later drove the disciples to reflect on the last miracle Jesus performed, and to see the care and involvement He has for His followers as they serve Him in the world.

Working

> After these things Jesus manifested Himself again to the disciples at the Sea of Tiberias; and He manifested Himself in this way. There were together Simon Peter, and Thomas called Didymus, and Nathanael of Cana in Galilee, and the sons of Zebedee, and two others of His disciples (John 21:1-2).

In the weeks since the Resurrection, the disciples' faith in Jesus had been vindicated. They discussed the Scriptures and thought about the future. And they talked about Jesus, wondering when they would see Him again. What would He say? What would He do? The possibilities were delicious. The stage was set for the Lord to illustrate His earthly ministry to the church.

As usual, Peter's inability to sit still helped create the scene. The aroma of the sea and the addictive rhythm of the lapping water were too much for Peter. Finally he blurted out to his companions, "I'm going fishing." The other disciples voiced their approval: "We will also come with you" (21:3). They went out and got into the boat; and that night they caught nothing.

The disciples were a microcosm of the church toiling in a restless world. The tiny boat bearing the apostolic band portrays some abiding realities important to our spiritual health.

First, a primary obligation of the church in the world is fishing or evangelism. Remember the scene of the first fishing miracle three years earlier? Jesus said, "Follow Me, and I will make you become fishers of men" (Mark 1:17). Evangelism is to have a prominent place in the ministry of the church. It is not to be eclipsed by social involvement, for if it is, the church will be in a dark day. We are facing that danger today. Recently, a Philippine Christian leader who pioneered the social witness of evangelical churches there voiced his fears for hard days ahead for evangelism. It used to be much easier, he said, to get money for evangelism than for social action. Now it is the reverse. The ideal, of course, is both. But history has shown how fragile the balance is. Let us never be lulled into giving evangelism second place.

Second, the picture before us suggests hard work. Fishing is exhausting labor which occupies people far into the night. In this picture, we are to realize that without Christ we can do nothing. Of course, the disciples were not as guilty in their fishing as we are in the reality of life-and-death evangelism. They paid careful attention to equipment and to strategy. And yet even to these "pros" the Lord said, "Apart from Me you can do nothing" (John 15:5).

It is so easy to become "professionals," to think that we can do spiritual work on our own, to think that if we are overloaded and busy, God will understand if we don't take time to seek His direction. And yet whatever is done in this way is nothing. We can witness and have it be nothing. We can donate hundreds of hours to the church and have it be nothing. We can preach and amount to nothing.

Learning

The night was now spent. The blush of dawn was warming the east and the disciples were tired and heading for home. They were probably not thinking of the Lord, and yet Jesus was watching them.

> But when the day was now breaking, Jesus stood on the beach; yet the disciples did not know that it was Jesus. Jesus therefore said to them, "Children, you do not have any fish, do you?"
> They answered Him, "No" (20:4-5).

It may have been the gloomy mists of dawn and their weariness that kept them from recognizing Him. Their only answer was, "No." And this is to their everlasting credit, as any fisherman will know. They admitted their failure. And in a spiritual sense, it is right here that salvation becomes possible. Malcolm Muggeridge has said that failure is the most creative phenomenon of life. If we did not fail, we would never make any progress. Failure demands that we assess our past methods to see what we have done right or wrong. Failure helps us discard the moribund and obsolete, and it opens us to new ideas.

Muggeridge says, "Christianity, from Golgotha onward, has been the sanctification of failure" (Ian Hunter, *Malcolm Muggeridge: A Life,* Thomas Nelson, p. 224). Our failures bring us face to face with the weaknesses and inadequacies that lie within us, so that God's strength is made perfect in weakness.

> We have this treasure in earthen vessels, that the surpassing greatness of the power may be of God and not from ourselves (2 Cor. 4:7).

It is in the breaking of these clay vessels that the riches of God are exposed for all to see. It is primarily our failures that create in us a poverty of spirit and thus make us fit receptacles for the blessings of the kingdom of God. But, we must admit our failures to receive the benefits. This is where the tragedy lies, because we naturally want to hide our inadequacies. We live in a society that has one unforgivable sin—failure. We live a tragedy of the greatest proportions when we will not admit even to ourselves that we have failed, whether it be in devotion to God, in relation to one another, or in our service.

One of the most serious faults of some Christian workers is to claim that souls are being saved when they are not; to assert their effectiveness when they are effete; to boast about their organization or church when they should be lamenting its failure; to loudly proclaim their effect on the world when the world doesn't know they exist.

How can Christ sanctify fantasy? The creative processes of the Holy Spirit that bring God's power are fully operative only when we admit exactly where we are, only when we own our failures as well as our successes. One of the abiding glories of the Gospel is that it brings us face to face with reality about ourselves and the world.

Christ knew that the disciples hadn't caught any fish. When He asked about their success and they admitted failure, He then could sanctify that failure.

And He said to them, "Cast the net on the right-hand side of the boat, and you will find a catch." They cast therefore, and then they were not able to haul it in because of the great number of fish. That disciple therefore whom Jesus loved said to Peter, "It is the Lord."

And so when Simon Peter heard that it was the Lord, he put his outer garment on (for he was stripped for work), and threw himself into the sea. But the other disciples came in the little boat, for they were not far from the land, but about one hundred yards away, dragging the net full of fish (21:6-8).

When John saw the net tighten with the great catch, he

looked toward shore and cried out, "It is the Lord." Then Peter was all action. Wanting to give the Lord a respectful greeting, he threw on his outer garment and performed a cannonball. People like Peter never just dive. At the first fish miracle three years before, Peter had been so awestruck that he had said, "Depart from me, for I am a sinful man, O Lord!" (Luke 5:8) Now, he not only understood his own sin but he also knew of God's grace. Arriving at the shore, he stood before Jesus, dripping wet, hair matted, and knowing that he was accepted.

Things were different now than before. The fishermen had found that it is Christ who brings the increase, and that apart from Him they could do nothing. They also knew that His resources were sufficient—whatever the catch. For with Christ directing the work, resources are never overstrained. Nothing, in a person or in a group, is beyond His power and grace.

Receiving

And so when they got out upon the land, they saw a charcoal fire already laid, and fish placed on it, and bread. Jesus said to them, "Bring some of the fish which you have now caught." Simon Peter went up, and drew the net to land, full of large fish, a hundred and fifty-three; and although there were so many, the net was not torn.

Jesus said to them, "Come and have breakfast." None of the disciples ventured to question Him, "Who are You?" knowing that it was the Lord. Jesus came and took the bread, and gave them, and the fish likewise (21:9-14).

There is something supernatural yet simple and uncomplicated here. The reason there is a mysterious air about this section of the Gospel is that it figuratively is a step into eternity. An event that happened 2,000 years ago pictures the church receiving her eternal reward. As Alexander Maclaren said:

All the details, such as the solid shore in contrast with the changeful sea, the increasing morning in contrast with the toilsome night, the feast prepared, have been from of old consecrated to shadow forth the differences between earth and heaven. It would be blindness not to see here a prophecy of the glad hour when Christ shall welcome to their home, amid the brightness of unsetting day, the souls that have served Him amidst the fluctuations and storms of life, and seen Him in its darkness, and shall satisfy all their desires with the "bread of heaven" (*Expositions of Holy Scripture,* vol. XI, Baker Book House, p. 356).

While we serve Him in this age on the dark seas of life, our risen Lord wants us to focus on the fact that He is on the eternal shore in the ever-increasing light, preparing a table for us.

He wants us to see that our works for Him are of eternal value. In encouraging His disciples to bring some of their catch, He showed that He accepted their service. And He added the result of their toil to the provision He already had prepared. He didn't need them, for He could have multiplied what He had. But He was teaching them—and us—that the believer's works follow him and are of eternal consequence. The smallest work done under the inspiration and direction of Christ is more enduring than the great monuments of our world. The essence of the eternal state is suggested by John's words, "It is the Lord." The knowledge of the Lord will be our increasing reward in life and through eternity. As the Apostle Paul said:

For now we see in a mirror dimly, but then face to face; now I know in part, but then I shall know fully just as I also have been fully known (1 Cor. 13:12).

As believers, we are all in the same boat, navigating the same waters. Though the waters are sometimes cold and harsh and stormy, all of us are to be involved in fishing, casting, and recasting our nets. As we face the realities of our lives, we need to say at times, "No, we have caught nothing." For it is this very failure that Christ can sanctify, if our focus is on Him.

> In the darkness, it is the Lord.
> In our failures, it is the Lord.
> In success, it is the Lord.

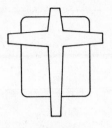

21
Loving and Following Christ
John 21:12-23

Cyrus the Great, King of Persia during the sixth century, had a general whose wife was suspected of treason. She was tried before the tribunal, found guilty, and sentenced to death. After the sentence was pronounced, the general made his way to Cyrus' throne and requested, "King Cyrus, please let me take her place."

Cyrus was in awe at what was transpiring before him and said to the court, "Can we terminate a love as great as this?"

He relaxed the sentence, paroling the woman to her husband. As the couple left the court, the general said to his wife, "Did you see the benevolent look in Cyrus' eyes as he changed the sentence?" His wife responded, "I only had eyes for the one who loved me enough to be willing to die for me."

Peter must have felt this kind of attraction to the risen Christ. His agony over his denial of Jesus has to be one of the most profound of all time. And so was his need of restoration. The pain of what he had done was still too firmly lodged in Peter's psyche, ready for instant replay.

Sure, there had been the Resurrection, the Lord's appearance, the comforting benediction, "Peace be with you." But Peter could not forget his lapse of love.

The night of fishing had been therapeutic for Peter, with the wind and water and expanse of sky. The miracle draught of fish was even more therapeutic. And now Peter stood dripping wet before the Lord, after his fully clothed plunge into the Sea of Tiberias. His desire to see Jesus was an impulsive demonstration of his love. But Peter was not healed. He had failed. He doubted his own fidelity. He wondered if he could ever again be used. He needed a touch from Christ, as we all do.

The fish breakfast on shore of the Sea of Tiberias evokes a timeless picture—the risen Lord with His back to the glistening blue morning sea, serving breakfast on the beach to the damp crew of disciples, while the smoke wafted between them. There was little conversation that morning. Things weren't the same as they had been before. The disciples were awkwardly silent as they sat huddled around the fire, gazing timidly at the Lord profiled against the morning mists that rose from Tiberias.

Restoration

When breakfast was finished, Jesus spoke to Peter: "Simon, son of John, do you love Me more than these?" (John 21:15) Peter's heart must have been pounding wildly. His stomach turned, his cheeks burned, and his eyes misted. He felt terrible. The Lord had really put it to him. "After all that has happened, Peter, can you truly say that you love Me? And do you love Me more than the other disciples do?"

Jesus addressed Peter as "Simon, son of John," his name before he met Christ. Jesus was intentionally calling into question his name as "Peter the rock." The message was, "Simon, you remember your human weakness, you know how you were before I met you."

When Jesus asked if Peter loved Him more than the other disciples did, Peter could not help but flash back to two weeks before in the Upper Room when he had said:

"Lord, where are You going?"
Jesus answered, "Where I go, you cannot follow Me now; but you shall follow later."
Peter said to Him, "Lord, why can I not follow You right now? I will lay down my life for You" (13:36-37).

Even though all may fall away because of You, I will never fall away (Matt. 26:33).

As Peter looked away from Jesus, his eyes fell on the charcoal fire on the beach, which was much like the charcoal fire in the hall where he had denied the Lord. His painful thoughts streamed forth with the aroma of the coals. "More than these, Simon?" "I will never fall away." "Do you love Me?" The Lord's question was like a knife spinning in the open wound.

Peter's answer to Jesus was, "Yes, Lord; You know that I love [have affection for] You" (21:15). Peter used *philia* for love, which means affection or friendship. He couldn't use *agape*, not with his feeling of failure and disgrace. Peter's presumption was gone.

With his confession of feelings of friendship for Christ, the Lord gave His charge, "Tend My lambs."

Jesus wasn't through, however. A second time He asked, "Simon, son of John, do you love Me?" (21:16) That is, "Simon, dropping all comparison, the unadorned question is, 'Do you really love Me?' This is the bottom line."

We can be sure that there was little movement as the smoke wafted above the apostolic band and Peter carefully and quietly answered, "Yes, Lord; You know I love [have affection for] You" (21:16). We must understand that Peter's answer was not bad. Paul used *philia* when he said, "If anyone does not have love [philia] for the Lord, let him be accursed. Maranatha" (1 Cor. 16:22). Friendship love is wonderful. But it wasn't enough for Peter. And yet Jesus' response to Peter's second confession of friendship was, "Shepherd My sheep."

There was a gracious violence in Jesus' questioning as He turned to Peter again and asked, "Simon, son of John, do you love [philia] Me?" This time the Lord assumed Peter's word.

In His first question, Jesus had challenged the superiority of Peter's love. In the second question He challenged whether Peter had any love at all. Now in this final question, He challenged Peter's claim to an affectionate love.

Peter was grieved at the question. And yet from that pain he steadfastly answered, "Lord, You know all things; You know that I love [affectionate, friendship love] You" (21:17). He threw himself on the Lord's perfect knowledge. He gave up on himself. "God, You know what I am, but I don't claim any more than that." Peter loved Jesus with the deepest of loves, but his illusions, his presumptions about himself were gone forever. And for the Lord, that was enough. He said, "Tend My sheep."

Love

As the restoration was accomplished in the sight of all, they understood that the Lord had planned this setting. Peter's denials were before a charcoal fire and now his confessions were before a charcoal fire. There were three denials, and now three confessions, as well as three commissions. This is significant because it was a Near Eastern custom to say something three times before witnesses in order to solemnize it (R. E. Brown, *The Gospel According to John* (xiii-xxi), Doubleday, p. 1112).

Through Peter Christ was saying to us all that the greatest priority in life is our love for God. In Peter we see a man who already loved God but who needed to be affirmed in that love before He could serve. The abiding principle for Peter and for us is that before all things, even before service to Him, we must love Him with all of our heart. This is the first question for every missionary, for every pastor, for every one who wants to please God.

It is all too easy in the everyday following of Christ to put the priority on service. Techniques and methods can easily become our primary focus. To carry out our methods we thirst for power. Instead of longing for and loving the source of the power, we lust simply for power alone. Production then becomes the center of our thinking and life is inverted. In their book, *We Would See Jesus,* Roy and Revel Hession say:

> To concentrate on service and activity for God may often actively thwart our attaining of the true goal, God Himself. At first sight it seems heroic to fling our lives away in the service of God and our fellows. We feel it is bound to mean more to Him than

our experience of Him. Service seems so unselfish, whereas concentrating on our walk with God seems selfish and self-centered.

But it is the very reverse. The things that God is most concerned about are our coldness of heart towards Himself and our proud, unbroken natures. Christian service of itself can, and so often does, leave our self-centered nature untouched. . . . With those things hidden in our hearts, we have only to work alongside others, and we find resentment, hardness, criticism, jealousy, and frustration issuing from our hearts. We think we are working for God, but the test of how little of our service is for Him is revealed by our resentment or self-pity, when the actions of others, or circumstances, or ill-health take it from us!

We need to leave our lusting for ever-larger spheres of Christian service and concentrate on seeing God for ourselves and finding the deep answer for life in Him (Christian Literature Crusade, pp. 14-15).

When the lawyer asked Jesus what was the greatest commandment, He answered:

"You shall love the Lord your God with all your heart, and with all your soul, and with all your mind. This is the great and foremost commandment" (Matt. 22:37-38).

This priority of love is demanding because it makes us face reality, as Peter did. As we reflect honestly on our lives, we too say, "Lord, You know all things" (21:17). In Peter's previous affirmations of Jesus' omniscience, he used a strong Greek word which meant that Jesus knew every detail. Now he switched to a word which meant intimate personal knowledge. It was as if he said, "Lord, You have walked with me. You know me personally in every way."

We too can bank on His intimate knowledge of what we are. As we become more honest in our love for Christ, He will affirm what is good in us and will challenge us to a higher plane. We will want to spend more time with Him because we love Him. This is the great test of our love for Christ, for we spend time with those whom we love.

Service

Jesus was not done with Peter. He now went on to speak to him about his service in the future. This came under two categories. Service for Christ would hold difficulties for Peter. And service for Christ would be uniquely fitted to the individual, so that there was no pattern for all the disciples. The important element in both the difficulty and the individuality of service was to follow Jesus.

• Difficulty. Jesus focused on the hardship of service by prophesying Peter's future:

> "Truly, truly, I say to you, when you were younger, you used to gird yourself, and walk wherever you wished; but when you grow old, you will stretch out your hands, and someone else will gird you, and bring you where you do not wish to go." Now this He said, signifying by what kind of death he would glorify God. And when He had spoken this, He said to him, "Follow Me!" (21:18-19)

While there are differing interpretations of this prophecy, I believe Jesus was saying that despite his aged infirmity, Peter would die a martyr's death by crucifixion. The giveaway is that John's description of Peter's death in verse 19, as something that would glorify God, used a phrase which was standard Christian language for martyrdom. The church fathers—including Iraeneus, Justin Martyr, and Cyprian—all viewed the phrase "you will stretch out your hands" as a description of crucifixion. We find this opinion also in the Epistles of Barnabas and the Didache (R.E. Brown, *The Gospel According* to John, vol. 2 (xiii-xxi), Doubleday, p. 1112). The sense of Christ's prophecy is: "When you were young, you had your own way. You girded yourself and went forth with conscious independence; but there is a future time coming when you will be infirm and someone else will gird you, and bind you and crucify you."

Every servant of Christ will discover that he must bear his own highly personal cross and at times experience some form of personal crucifixion. This was dramatically vivid in the early years of the Salvation Army. When William Booth began his mission work in East London in 1865, he met violent opposition that grew even more intense in 1878 when his Christian Mission became the Salvation Army and Booth assumed the title of General. The Army's historians tell us:

> One Salvation Army officer came into a meeting loaded down with dead cats and rats; he explained these had been thrown at him; and that he caught and held the dead animals because if he dropped them the crowd would merely pick them up to be thrown again. Pots of human urine were often dumped on the street preachers. Beatings were not uncommon; in 1889, at least 669 Salvation Army members were assaulted—some were killed and many were maimed. Even children were not immune; hoodlums threw lime in the eyes of a child of a Salvation Army member. The newspapers ridiculed Booth. *Punch* referred to him as "Field Marshal von Booth." Soon a bunch of thugs and ruffians organized themselves into the "Skeleton Army" and devoted themselves to disrupting the meetings of the Salvation Army. They often attacked Salvation Army members as they paraded through the streets or held open-air meetings. They frequently stormed Salvation Army meeting halls by the hundreds, broke out the windowpanes, and wrecked the inside of buildings. At first the police did little to stop the "Skeleton Army." Instead of helping they frequently harassed Booth and his followers (William Booth, *Twenty Centuries of Great Preaching*, vol. 5, Word Books, p. 204).

In his book, *The General Next to God,* William Collier writes:

> Neither age nor sex proved a barrier for the mobs were out for blood. In Northampton, one blackguard tried to knife a passing lassie; Wolverhampton thugs flung lime in a Salvationist child's eyes. At Hastings, Mrs. Susannah Beaty, one of Booth's first converts on Mile End Waste, became the Army's first martyr, buried from Clapton's Congress Hall. Reeling under a fire of rocks and putrid fish, she was kicked deliberately in the womb and left for dead in a dark alley of the Old Town. The doctor's prophecy that her injuries could prove fatal came appallingly true.

The since-revised dedication of the 'eighties involved stern and binding promises—"You must be willing that the child should spend all its life in the Salvation Army, wherever God should choose to send it, that it should be despised, hated, cursed, beaten, kicked, imprisoned, or killed for Christ's sake" (E.P. Dutton, pp. 108-109).

Why did the early Salvationists become as the offscouring of the earth? Why was it that Peter came to such a difficult end? The answer is inherent in Paul's words to the Corinthians:

For the love of Christ controls us, having concluded this, that one died for all, therefore all died; and he died for all, that they who live should no longer live for themselves, but for Him who died and rose again on their behalf (2 Cor. 5:14-15).

When the love of Christ controls a person, he no longer lives for himself but for Christ alone. The word for control that Paul used is translated variously in the New Testament. Sometimes it speaks of one who is "pressed in spirit" (Acts 18:5, KJV). Other times it is used to describe the tight hold that men keep on a prisoner (Luke 22:63). The idea behind the word is "to be gripped or hemmed in." Christ's love so grips His followers and hems them in that they can do nothing but live for Him!

Someone once introduced Hudson Taylor as a great missionary who had given his life to the Orient because he loved the Chinese. Taylor slowly shook his head and answered thoughtfully, "No, not because I loved the Chinese, but because I loved God." The love of Christ controlled him.

The controlling love of Christ will mean suffering for the servant of Christ. When Ananias was sent to the newly-converted Saul of Tarsus, he went with this message from the Lord:

"Go, for he is a chosen instrument of Mine, to bear My name before the Gentiles and the kings and sons of Israel; for I will show him how much he must suffer for My name's sake" (Acts 9:15-16).

And when Paul was a prisoner in Rome, he wrote to the church at Philippi: "For to you it has been granted for Christ's sake, not only to believe in Him, but also to suffer for His sake" (Phil. 1:29).

If our lives are characterized by ease, if we incur no problems because of our Christianity, there is every likelihood that something is wrong. The British preacher, John Stott, preaching on 2 Corinthians 5 at Urbana Missionary Convention in 1970, said:

> Now the church is not persecuted so much as ignored. Its revolutionary message has been reduced to a toothless creed for bourgeois suburbanites. Nobody opposes it any longer, because really there is nothing to oppose.
>
> My own conviction, for what it is worth, is that if we Christians were to compromise less, we would undoubtedly suffer more. If we were to hold fast the old-fashioned Gospel of Christ crucified for sinners, and of salvation as an absolutely free and undeserved gift, then the Cross would again become a stumbling block to the proud.
>
> If we were to maintain the high moral standards of Jesus—of uncorruptible honesty and integrity, of chastity before marriage and fidelity in it, and of costly, self-sacrificial love, then there would be a public outcry that the church had returned to Puritanism.
>
> If we were to dare once more to talk plainly about the alternatives of life and death, salvation and judgment, heaven and hell, then the world would rise up in anger against such "old-fashioned rubbish."
>
> Physical violence, imprisonment and death may not be the fate of Christians in the West today, but faithfulness to Jesus Christ shall without doubt bring ridicule and ostracism. This should not surprise us, however, for we are followers of the suffering Christ (John Stott, *Focus on Christ,* London Fount Paperbacks, p. 135).

Christ wanted Peter to know that if he was going to truly serve Him, he would experience difficulty. And that is what He wants us to know also. But in this difficulty, His challenge to Peter—and to us—is, "Follow Me."

• Individuality. As Jesus and Peter were talking, they must have left the fire and begun walking together. For when Jesus prophesied of Peter's suffering, Peter turned around to John who was close behind and asked Jesus, "Lord, and what about this man?" (21:21)

Good old Peter! He loved Jesus with all his heart. He had been restored. He had been commissioned. But he was still Peter. Jesus answered, "If I want him to remain until I come, what is that to you? You follow Me!" (21:22) "Don't concern yourself, Peter, with what I choose to do in the lives of My other servants. You just be sure you are following Me."

Jesus was not suggesting that Peter should be disinterested in the welfare of others. Rather, He wanted to discourage the unhealthy tendency to measure himself by other people. There is a passage in C.S. Lewis' *The Horse and His Boy* which beautifully illustrates this point. The boy, Shasta, is conversing with the Christ figure, the lion Aslan. Aslan is recounting his sovereign workings in Shasta's life, how that he was the lion who drove the jackals away while Shasta slept and comforted him among the houses of the dead and propelled the boat which bore him to the shore to receive help. As Shasta listened, reflecting on the lion's sovereign claims, he suddenly questioned:

"Then it was you who wounded Aravis?"
"It was I."
"But what for?"
"Child," said the Voice, "I am telling your story, not hers. I tell no one any story but his own" (Collins, 1954, p. 147).

Each of us as a sovereign creation of God has worth and a place in God's plan. God's favor in our lives is not to be determined by comparison with others. We are not to involve ourselves in unprofitable musings about the relative providences of our lives—how one brother has it easier than another; or how one ministry is filled with hardship and another is not; or why one becomes famous and another is obscured. Each of us is simply to follow Christ.

No matter where we are in life, His call is, "Follow Me." If you are a new Christian, this is Christ's abiding command and you are asked to respond at your own level of understanding. If you have been through the wars of Christian service, it is perhaps infinitely more complex for your mind, and yet just as simple in its call for obedience.

We too stand on the eastern shore of the Sea of Tiberias. A gentle morning breeze freshens our faces and tiny waves run up on the sand with a silvery ripple and then die on the shore. A fishing boat has been drawn up on the deserted shore, its nets unbroken although they have held a great haul. Near us we see the remnants of the fishermen's breakfast and the dying embers of a coal fire.

And as we listen we hear His words, not only lingering on the beach but speaking to our hearts:

> "Do you love Me?"
> "Feed My sheep."
> "Follow Me."

In devotion to our Lord who loved us enough to die for us, let us follow Him with a love that eloquently speaks of who He is—our Saviour and our King.